The Word of truth

The Word of truth

Scripture — its origin, sufficiency and relevance

Robert J. Sheehan

EVANGELICAL PRESS

EVANGELICAL PRESS
Grange Close, Faverdale North Industrial Estate, Darlington,
Co. Durham, DL3 0PH, England

First published 1998

British Library Cataloguing in Publication Data available

ISBN 0 85234 410 4

Printed and bound in Great Britain by Creative Print & Design Wales,
Ebbw Vale

Contents

Robert J. Sheehan
(1951-1997)

Robert Sheehan was brought up in Barking, Essex, in a Christian family. His parents, who became Christians soon after his birth, were active members of New Park Hall, where his father was a deacon and both were involved in the work of the Sunday School. They were very regular in their attendance at services and it was a rarity for them to miss a prayer meeting. Bob himself was converted through the preaching of Rev. Ron Burton and was baptized while still in his early teens. Together with his brother Leslie, he was soon involved in the Covenanters' group and young people's work.

On leaving school, Bob wished to go into hospital administration but when he went for an interview he was told to go to university and gain a degree — in any subject he liked! He therefore decided to study theology at London Bible College. During his first year at the college, having only preached once before, he was approached by the principal and asked if he would like to become student pastor at a small village chapel in Buckinghamshire. His second year at LBC therefore saw him travelling each Friday to Hyde Heath — which involved a ride on the underground followed by a three-mile cycle-ride, on a bicycle loaned by the church secretary. In addition to visitation and leading the Bible Study and prayer meeting on Fridays, he was also involved in preaching twice on Sundays and in leading the young people's Bible Study. From this work, Bob felt that the Lord was calling him into the full-time ministry.

On completion of his London University degree, Bob was called to the pastorate of a Baptist church in Coventry. He accepted, believing the church to be an evangelical one. However, he quickly found that this was not the case and, although a few Christians there loved the truth, the majority of the membership, including all the church officers, rejected the preaching. After only a year, Bob resigned and the church asked him to leave forthwith.

Through the kindness of an old college friend, Bob and his family were then allowed the use of the manse of Townley Road Strict Baptist Church in Bexleyheath, Kent. At this time the door also opened for Bob to teach at a girls' school in Plumstead, London.

Bob's arrival at Bexleyheath also coincided with an outreach of the church to a group of sixth-formers from a local grammar school. He was able to discuss the topic of creation versus evolution with them and, one by one, they were converted. One member of this group is now himself a pastor, another a missionary and others active church officers.

Opportunity was also given to Bob to preach at the church in Bexleyheath and in 1974 they called him to the pastorate. The Lord blessed his ministry and a number of people were brought to salvation.

During his time at Bexleyheath, in addition to preaching and pastoring, Bob became an Assistant Editor of *Grace Magazine*, joined the Council of the Strict Baptist Mission (now the Grace Baptist Mission) and the Metropolitan Association of Strict Baptist Churches. He was also given the opportunity to speak at a number of conferences and to write articles for *Grace Magazine* and *Reformation Today*. He gave lectures in his home on Theology and New Testament Greek, which were attended by a number of men, some of whom were themselves pastors. He was appointed as one of the trustees of the Evangelical Library in London, eventually becoming Chairman in 1996.

At the beginning of 1980, Bob felt that his time at Bexleyheath was drawing to a close, that he could lead the church no further. During that summer he was a preacher at the Carey Family Conference and while there was invited to preach at Welwyn Evangelical Church. This he did and was subsequently asked to lead a series of midweek meetings at the church on the subject of the work of the Holy Spirit in the Old Testament. Shortly afterwards Bob was called to the pastorate of this church, a position which he took up in January 1982 and was to hold until his death in 1997.

At the time of his appointment, the European Missionary Fellowship had only recently moved their headquarters to Welwyn, and the Rev. T. Omri Jenkins, who was then the General Secretary of the mission, asked Bob if he would lecture in Systematic Theology at their School of Evangelism. This was later extended to include New Testament Greek. He also gave lectures at the London Theological Seminary — receiving a further invitation to lecture there shortly before his death — and at the London Reformed Baptist Seminary.

Bob was convinced that there was a great need for men who were considering going into the ministry to have theological training and, along with Pastor Stan Evers of Potton, commenced a monthly Saturday morning seminary, which was attended by about twenty men from Hertfordshire, Bedfordshire and Buckinghamshire. During the course of his ministry at Welwyn a number of men from the membership of the church were called into the ministry and all of them testify to Bob's encouragement and help.

In all the churches he pastored, Bob preached systematically through books of the Bible, except for church holidays, when he would often choose to preach on a theme. He also laid great emphasis on pastoral work and sought to visit church members regularly. He saw missionary work as an important part of the life of the church and his zeal was passed on to the membership of Welwyn Evangelical Church. He liked to be personally involved in overseas work supported by the church and regularly visited missionaries in Argentina and Spain. In between visits he kept in close contact with them by telephone.

Towards the end of his life, Bob was much in demand for preaching at conferences or in other churches and also as a writer. He was gifted with a very active mind which meant that he was able to memorize passages from Scripture and other books that he read, and to preach and lecture using brief notes containing a few headings and cross-references. The Lord was pleased to bless his ministry and many, both in his home church and further afield, continue to give thanks to God for all the help and blessings they have received as a result of it. He leaves a widow and four children, all of whom are believers.

Wendy Sheehan
April 1998

Preface

It has been my privilege for many years to give lectures in Systematic Theology to many students from different parts of Europe and the world at the European Missionary Fellowship School of Evangelism. Over the past few years my friend Erroll Hulse has published a number of these lectures in his bi-monthly magazine *Reformation Today*. This book consists of those articles revised with some additional material which has not up till now appeared in print.

In days when there is widespread defection from the historic Reformed doctrine of Scripture and, particularly, a rejection of the sufficiency of Scripture, I hope that these writings will make some small contribution to a reaffirmation of this all-important doctrine. A false doctrine of Scripture leads inexorably to the establishment of alternative authorities to that of the inspired Word of God. While one leading modernist recently asserted that the greatest danger to the church of Christ in the modern world was a return to the Bible, it is my firm conviction that only confidence in an inspired, infallible, inerrant, authoritative and sufficient Bible can restore the glory of God to the church of Christ.

R. J. Sheehan
Welwyn
1997

What is theology?

Everything a theologian does in the church contributes to the spread of the knowledge of God and the salvation of men.

Martin Luther

If you think that you know all that you need to know, you are already like a full bottle that will hold no more.

Richard Baxter

The person who addresses himself to the interpretation and formulation of the truth conveyed to us by revelation is destitute of the prime requisite if he is not imbued with the humility and enlightenment which the indwelling of the Holy Spirit imparts.

John Murray

1.
What is theology?

The term defined

In ancient Greece every story with the gods as its theme was a theology, and every writer about the gods, however fanciful, absurd, obscene or serious, was a theologian! There were theologies and theologians by their hundreds, speculating, imagining, mocking and idealizing to their hearts' content. It is tempting to think, in the modern world, that this definition has been reintroduced! We are surrounded by the shifting shadows of human speculation.

It was inevitable that serious-minded men would not long allow theology to be the property of the tellers of fairy tales. Aristotle, the philosopher (385-324 B.C), with his strong idea of a first cause, or prime mover, on which the whole process of cosmic development depended, saw theology as the study of being and existence. He rescued theology, as a concept, from the fevered imaginations of the storytellers and narrowed it to the speculative theories of the philosophers. Theology became intellectually respectable, and irrelevant to the masses.

The incarnation of the Son of God brought about a Christian interest in theology. To the early Church Fathers, however, theology was an interest in the person of Christ, his deity and nature. Hippolytus (A.D. *c*. 170 - *c*. 236), a keen controversialist over Christology, argued that Christ had been 'theologized' from the earliest days. The interest of John's Gospel and epistles in the person of Christ gained for John the title 'John the theologian'. Theology was equivalent to Christology, the study of who Jesus is and, in particular, concentrated on his divine nature rather than his human.

With Abelard (1079-1143) we enter on the modern use of the term 'theology'. It was the study of the truths of religion in general. The being and existence of God are included, as is Christology, but far more also. The whole realm of religion became the study of theology.

The definition of theology as the study of religion is, however, inadequate and misleading. 'Religion' is a very wide term. It refers to widely varying views. A study of religion could include all the ancient Greek theologies and those of other nations too, all the speculations of philosophers, all the religions of the world and all the interpretations of men with regard to religious ideas. A study of religion tends to be an investigation into human beliefs, all man's erroneous ideas and speculations, as well as any truth which may exist.

In the modern world religious studies tend to be comparative religions, philosophical speculations, the study of human ideas of spirituality and religiosity. Most religion is man-made and man-centred and, therefore, not the proper subject for theology, which is God-centred.

Later writers have defined theology as the study of faith. However, this definition suffers from the same weakness as the previous one. Faith is subjective; truth is objective. A study of faith is man-centred, what man believes about God. As there are so many views of God, it is evident that most are wrong. Truth is one; error takes many forms. True theology cannot be a study of what man thinks; otherwise it is no different from philosophy. It would only reveal man, not God.

There can only be one theology, one truth about God. Theology must be the study of God insofar as God has revealed himself to man. Theology is not the study of man's speculations. It is the study of God's self-revelation.

For theology to be possible, three things must be true.

Firstly, *there must be a God* about whom there can be facts.

Secondly, *this God must have made himself known to man.* Revelation must take place. An unrevealed God is an unknown God. What is not revealed can only be the object of speculation and can never have the certainty to be a fact. Without revelation, philosophy, religion and faith are possible, but all as uncertifiable human activities. No revelation means no theology. If there is no revelation, there can be no facts about God.

Thirdly, *man must have the ability to receive this revelation, understand it and use it.* Man has to have religious and rational capacities. A revelation which could not be received, understood and applied would be useless and would not be a revelation, but a hiding of God. A man who transmitted a programme without allowing anyone to receive it would be mocking them and himself. In the same way, a God who gives revelation must do so with the intention of enabling man to receive it. Theology is the study of revealed truth about God. The Christian, as we shall see, believes that the revelation that God has given is accurately recorded in the Bible. Theology is, therefore, the study of the Bible as an infallible record of God's revelation.

Proper attitudes to theology

For the moment we shall assume that God exists, that he has revealed facts about himself and that man is able to receive and understand these facts — i.e. we shall assume the possibility of theology. What attitudes ought we to have towards this revelation?

1. We are recipients of revelation, not judges of it

A botanist may not like the colour, smell, shape or texture of every flower he studies, but he would far exceed his authority as a scientist if he asked for the removal of a species from the catalogues of flora because of his taste and prejudice! The botanist must study the flowers that exist, and not decide which he would prefer to be non-existent. Scientific procedure requires the study of the facts, not the elimination of facts that are disliked.

In the same way, man must study theology not as a judge, ignoring what he finds distasteful and unacceptable in God's revelation and only accepting what suits his prejudices, but accepting the revelation as it is. He may not change the revelation because he dislikes it. The function of the theologian is to study what God has revealed, not to express his own prejudices. When he moves from revealed facts to his own prejudices, he has moved from the proper subject of theology — revealed facts — to his subjective opinions — in other words, to personal religion.

If we may change the analogy from the botanist to the journalist, we may again see why the theologian may not be a judge, but only a reporter of facts. How often we hear the complaint that a journalist, after an interview, printed a report that was not based on the interview at all! When a reporter adds to and subtracts from the interview to make the conversation more sensational and newsworthy, he is looked on with disdain by those who value the truth. The theologian completely exceeds his mandate, and shows a considerable degree of arrogance in the process, when he listens to what God reveals and decides that it needs to be tampered with by him before it can be passed on. He should not manufacture ideas. He is only to analyse and explain truth.

From botanists and journalists we turn to physicists. Faced with the need to define light, physicists describe it in terms of waves and particles, yet accept these two as irreconcilable descriptions. Physicists then plead antinomy — that is, two truths, which are apparently contradictory, yet held together in tension. To deny the presence of antinomy in many areas of knowledge would simply be to turn a blind eye to the facts. In the revelation of God there are antinomies — truths which we cannot see a way of reconciling — but to admit the existence of antinomies in the divine revelation is a much more honourable course than to eliminate one side of the antimony, or to accuse God of being irrational. God is three but one. Christ is human and divine. God is sovereign and man is responsible. We know this because God has revealed it. The theologian may not deny it because he cannot explain it!

When man sets himself up as the judge of God's revelation, wanting to act as its editor and to reconstruct it according to his own prejudices, he is merely demonstrating his own arrogance, denying the finitude of his mind and setting himself up in the place of God. Such a man is not a theologian; he is a humanist.

2. Our understanding of revelation is never perfect

It is one thing to have a perfect revelation, but entirely another to have a perfect understanding of that revelation. No one does. It ought to be a first principle of every theologian that as God has given the revelation his help should be sought in understanding it. Who would not seek an artist's help in understanding his own paintings, or an author's aid in interpreting his book? Can the Revealer's aid be ignored in interpreting his revelation?

However humbly and reverently a man seeks to interpret God's revelation, however much he might try to avoid questionable meanings and sectarian nuances, there is a degree of human subjectivity and frailty in all interpretation. Two principles, therefore, need to guide him which themselves require to be held in tension.

Firstly, he must not come to interpret the revelation bound by the traditions of the past. A traditional interpretation can be important and correct, but it can be hopelessly wrong. Time-honoured traditions can be traditional errors. The history of Roman Catholicism proves it.

Secondly, he must not come to the revelation with contempt for the interpretations of others. There is a horrible conceit in thinking that only I have properly understood a truth and all others have been ignorant and misled. New ideas in theology are usually wrong. The history of the cults proves it.

Humility requires the theologian to seek the help of God, and the help of others who have sought God's aid, in understanding his revelation. Self-sufficiency is disastrous in theology.

3. We must use the revelation for the purposes for which it was given

We are called to be theologians, not theoreticians. The theologian is always in danger of studying God's revelation as an academic exercise. There is no benefit at all in knowledge *about* God that does not lead to knowledge *of* God. We would find it very strange if someone devoted his life to the study of a man and yet showed no interest in ever meeting him. So with the theologian and God! Theology must not simply be the study of what has come from God, but must lead us to him.

While theology must not be confused with religion and faith, it is to result in them. It is obscene that a creature should receive a revelation from his Creator and simply show a theoretical, intellectual interest in it. It is as if a child were to receive a gift but never take off the wrapping paper and simply looked at the box without ever opening it.

There are also theological theoreticians of another sort. They use God's revelation as a springboard for their own speculations. God, it seems, has not revealed enough for them. They must pry into hidden things and speculate about the unknown. This is a high form of contempt for God's revelation. It is as if a man had taken down a large Bible from a bookshelf, not to read it, but to stand on it to increase his height to look out of a high window!

Theoretical speculation is not theology. It is philosophy. Unapplied revelation is not theology. It is theory. Unless God's revelation sets the bounds for our thinking and the rules for our living, it is misused.

Approaches to theology

As theology is the study of the facts revealed by God about himself and his relationship to all else, there are two areas of study related to theology proper. At one end of theological study we have apologetics, the study of the rational arguments by which it is demonstrated that it is reasonable to believe in God and a revelation from him. At the other end we have historical theology, the study of the history of the interpretation of the revelation over the centuries after the revelation was given. Apologetics asks, 'Is it reasonable for man to believe in this revelation?' Historical theology asks, 'How have men interpreted this revelation?'

Theology proper has traditionally been divided into four parts. Regrettably they have often been seen as four distinct disciplines. In fact, they are one discipline divided into four related parts. No one part is complete without the other. A lack of any part introduces distortion and imbalance.

1. God's revelation must be studied exegetically

Every word, sentence, paragraph, section, etc., needs careful study in its nearer and wider contexts. Some of the best theologians began as professors of exegesis. The theology of the revelation can only arise from the form in which it was given. Exegetical theology demands detailed study of the revelation in the form in which it was given.

2. It must be studied chronologically

Chronological theology (or biblical theology as it is sometimes called, but this is a misnomer) takes into account the fact that God did not give his revelation all at once, but over a period of time. He gradually made his character and ways known. Chronological theology traces the progress of this divine unveiling.

3. It must be studied thematically

The sum total of all that is taught on a particular aspect of God's self-revelation needs to be grasped, and each separate theme needs to be related to each other theme. This whole view of teaching, in its parts and in its totality, is the province of systematic theology.

4. It needs to be applied to the modern situation

Having discovered what the truth is, we need to apply it. This is practical theology. It is the purpose to which all the other parts of theology are contributing and leading.

All this may be illustrated by reference to a cardigan, or jumper. Let us imagine a man is wearing a highly patterned jumper. We may look at details in the pattern (an exegetical study). We may consider how it looked when ten rows had been knitted, then when fifty and a hundred had been completed (a chronological study). We may look at the finished article in its parts — sleeves, front, back or as a whole (a systematic study). We may put it on to keep warm (a practical study). Together the four studies will give us a whole picture. Any one will give only a partial picture.

The tendencies that have existed to make the four parts of theology rivals, or distinct disciplines, ought to be avoided. Each needs each other if imbalance is to be avoided. In all its parts, the one theology which comes from the study of one revelation of the one true and living God has much to teach us that we need to know. While no one has a full understanding of theology, no one should decide that theology is not for him. Theology is the study of what God has revealed to us for our present and eternal benefit. This revelation has been given in the Bible.

A self-revealing God

Some men deny the Infinite; some, too, deny the sun; they are the blind.

Victor Hugo

Every atheist is a grand fool. If he were not a fool, he would not imagine a thing so contrary to the stream of universal reason in the world, contrary to the natural dictates of his own soul, and contrary to the testimony of every creature and link in the chain of creation.

Stephen Charnock

If God be a person, it follows by stringent necessity that he can be known only as far as he reveals or expresses himself.

Benjamin Warfield

2.
A self-revealing God

Theology is the study of the revelation that God has caused to be recorded in the Bible. Theology is only possible because of the existence of God. But how do we know that God exists? Is the fact of God's existence something that has to be proved, is it known intuitively, or is it learned?

Scriptural examples

When we turn to the Scriptures we have a number of examples of preaching. It is evident that when the prophets, our Lord, or the apostles addressed God's people, they made no attempt to prove his existence. This is to be expected because such a proof would be unnecessary. The same is true in preaching addressed to religious Jews and God-fearing Gentiles in the synagogues.

More significant, however, are the examples of preaching to heathen congregations. Here again there is no attempt to prove God's existence. In addressing the fanatical crowd at Lystra, Paul proclaimed the living God, the Creator, the Ruler of history, the long-suffering God who had left a witness to himself (Acts 14:15-17). God was proclaimed in his works; it was not a question of proving his existence.

In the less frenzied context of his speech to the Athenian philosophers, Paul proclaimed to them the unknown God, the Creator and Sustainer of all things, on whom everything depends, the forbearing God who demands repentance of a world he will judge (Acts 17:22-33). Again the acts of God were declared, rather than the existence of God being demonstrated.

When we consider the biblical books themselves, the same conclusion is reached. In the Old Testament the existence of God is presupposed. In the New Testament it is assumed.

Why does Scripture presuppose God's existence?

The *fact* that God's existence is a basic presupposition in biblical preaching and writing can hardly be disputed. The reasons for this are variously understood and need to be considered. We shall consider three main interpretations.

1. Atheism was virtually unknown in biblical times

It has been asserted that consistent atheism is a modern phenomenon, with its rise in the seventeenth century and its widespread influence in the eighteenth century, 'the Age of Reason'. Before then atheism was a minority interest. The Puritan Stephen Charnock reckoned that there were only about twenty professed atheists recorded in world history before his day. Everyone believed in God in biblical times and in the centuries that followed. There was, therefore, no need to prove God's existence in the context in which the Scriptures were written and their message preached. God's existence could be presupposed because everyone accepted it.

There is, however, a fundamental flaw in this line of reasoning. It treats the ancient belief in *gods*, which cannot be denied, as synonymous with belief in *God*. To biblical thinking this would have been a dreadful and blasphemous equation. It is also an entirely false equation. Why should a worshipper of the god Chemosh presuppose the existence of the God Jehovah? On what basis does a person believing in one god automatically accept the existence of another? Do Christians who believe in God the Father automatically presuppose the existence of Allah?

It is the constant concern of the scriptural writers and preachers to set a distance between the one true and living God and the counterfeit, man-made gods who are created by men as substitutes for him. With what ferocity the psalmist rages against idols of silver and gold and contrasts them with the sovereign God of heaven! (Ps. 115:2-8). Isaiah unleashes an indignant tirade against idols, which are 'nothing', and contrasts them with the only true God (Isa. 44:6-20). With what clarity the apostles call men from the worship of vain and worthless idols, 'so-called' gods, to serve the living and true God! (Acts 14:15; 1 Thess. 1:9; 1 Cor. 8:4-6).

The biblical division between the true God and the counterfeit gods is clear. The scriptural writers and preachers were concerned that their hearers and readers should leave the counterfeits and worship the true God. They did not suggest that all men worship the same God under different names, but that false gods should be forsaken for the true God. Those who did not know God and were without God and without hope needed to come to a knowledge of him (Gal. 4:8; Eph. 2:12).

The presupposition that God exists which pervades biblical writing and preaching cannot be explained on the grounds that all men believed in God in those days. They did not. Only a small minority believed in God in biblical times, as in ours; the rest believed in gods of their own making.

2. The Bible was written to the believing community

A great change has overtaken the theory of Bible translation in the twentieth century. In some circles the Bible reader is now more important than the Bible writer. The reader whose attention the translator is concerned to win is the non-Christian. The Bible is viewed as God's message to sinful man.

In reaction to this, and in accordance with earlier theories of translation, other translators have felt it necessary to emphasize that the recipients of the original Bible books were not unbelievers, but covenant communities — Israel and the churches. The Bible is God's message to saved men.

Both of these views affect our discussion. If the Bible is written to non-Christians then it would seem that under no circumstances did the writers feel it necessary to prove God's existence. They simply declared what he had done to an unbelieving audience. If, however, the Bible is written to Christians, the writers would have felt no need to prove God's existence to believers.

Neither of these views is correct. Some parts of the Bible were evidently written to non-Christians, to encourage them to believe. John clearly states in his Gospel that his purpose was evangelistic (John 20:30-31). Other sections, such as the epistles, were addressed to believing churches, the saints in a particular place. Their purpose was to strengthen and establish the faith of believers (e.g. Phil. 1:1-2; 1 John 5:13).

When a comparison is made between the didactic sections addressed to believers and the evangelistic passages addressed to unbelievers, no difference can be found in the presuppositions relating to God's existence. The epistle to the Hebrews, written to exhort believers to faithfulness, begins with an affirmation of God's actions. The Gospel of John, written to unbelievers, begins by relating the Word to God. Neither seeks to prove his existence.

It may not, therefore, be argued that the Bible presupposes the existence of God because it was written to people who already believed in the God of the Bible. Not all of it was.

3. All men have a sense of God in their hearts

There are in Scripture three strands of teaching that suggest that no man is *naturally* an atheist. He may choose to become an atheist, or divert his knowledge of the true God so as to worship a substitute, but all men have a God-given sense of God. This God-consciousness is due to the following causes.

God's self-revelation as Creator (Ps. 19:1-6; Rom. 1:18-22)

The psalmist asserts that the heavens declare the glory of God. The Hebrew term he uses for 'glory' contains the idea of weight, or heaviness. The weight of something often gives it significance. No one minds a snowflake falling on his head, but few would be happy to be hit by a falling chimney-stack! Weight lends significance! The heavens declare God's 'weight'; they proclaim his significance. Why he is important has to be noted.

Of course, it is not just the heavens that reveal his importance, but everything that God has created. Paul declares that God has been revealing himself through created things for as long as they have existed.

God himself is invisible, but through the things he has created he can, and does, reveal some of his character and significance. He reveals his eternal power. Through my study window I see grass, trees, fields, a river, clouds, rain, horses, humans, dogs, etc. All are very different, complex and varied, and all provide evidence of the power of their Creator and require the conclusion that the Creator must have existed before the creation.

The sight of variety, colour, complexity, simplicity — the whole range of creation — not only reveals eternal power but divinity. God, not in essence, but in creative action, is awesome. So much is fearfully and wonderfully made! Here in creation is a call to worship, to bring glory, praise and honour to the Creator.

It is not, however, creation itself that requires man to acknowledge God's eternal power and deity. Creation, or the much-praised 'Mother Nature', has no power to reveal God of itself. It is God himself who makes himself known. Through the things that are made, God is continually and actively revealing himself. Creation is God's autobiography. Every day in nature's round is a new page of divine self-revelation.

God does not reveal himself obscurely, but plainly. He makes clear what is known of God. The recipients of this revelation are *all men*. The sphere of the revelation is as all-embracing as the sun. Man is left in no doubt. God makes himself known to men in creation, and they know God. They may suppress this revelation, deny it, distort it, reinterpret it, or do whatever they will with it. However, God's self-revelation in creation means that no one is naturally an atheist, nor even an agnostic. Human 'ignorance' of God is culpable, not respectable! It is the rejection of revealed knowledge.

God's self-revelation in man's nature (Rom. 1:32; 2:12-16)

None of God's creatures is more fearfully and wonderfully made than man. It is not, however, his physical attributes which are most astonishing, but his moral powers. Unlike any other creature, man, male and female, is made in the image of God (Gen. 1:26-27). This image may well include his role of dominion over creation, his societal nature and many other aspects of his essential humanity, but undoubtedly it includes his mental and moral faculties (Eph. 4:24; Col. 3:10).

Men who have never heard of the Bible, and know nothing about Moses or Christ, are not entirely ignorant of the will of God for them. They do not have the law as it was revealed to Israel, either in its longer forms throughout the Pentateuch, or in its summary form, the Ten Commandments, but they do have 'the work of the law written in their hearts'. In Jewish idiom, 'to work the work of God' is to do what God requires (John 6:28-29). Therefore, to have the work of the law written in the heart is to have the requirements of the law written there. All men, Gentiles as well as Jews, have an inward knowledge of God's legal requirements.

We need not be in any doubt as to what these legal requirements are. Our Lord not only told us what the first and second greatest commands in God's law are, but he also said that the whole of the Old Testament revelation hangs on them (Matt. 22:37-40). They are the foundational principles of this revelation and its supreme duties.

All men have an inner sense that they ought to love God. Men are 'naturally' religious. All men have an inner sense of duty towards their fellow humans. They have a concept of 'natural' justice and 'natural' affection. Even avowed atheists cannot help revealing themselves as theists sometimes. The story is told of an atheist who avowed, 'I do not believe in God or any such idea. God is my witness!' We remember that concentration camp commandants were often affectionate family men. Even cannibals usually refuse to eat close relatives and friends! There is an inner duty to God and man that it is very hard to erase. We are not naturally irreligious and amoral.

God has given our inner religious and moral sense two allies: conscience and thoughts. Conscience works on our sensitivities and emotions, creating fear of the consequences of wrongdoing and regret at evil committed. Our thoughts reason with us about the rightness or wrongness of our actions.

Some may wish to suggest that man is a highly developed amoeba, a refined ape, or the residue of a primeval soup, but the Christian is required to address men as essentially religious and moral beings. They may loudly proclaim their atheism and liberation from the restraints of conscience, but big claims are often ignorant and empty boasts.

The fundamental fact of theism

If, as we have asserted, all men know that there is a Creator God, eternally powerful and worthy of worship, and all men have a religious and moral sense of duty, why do so many claim to be atheists?

Firstly, it needs to be recognized that, even as we approach the twenty-first century, vast numbers of human beings do not claim to be atheists. They claim to worship God. They do see themselves as religious and they do maintain a morality. Their problem is that the gods they worship are not gods at all.

Paul tells us that from their earliest days men with futile, foolish, wicked hearts turned from the worship of the invisible, true and living God to worship gods which were visible and acceptable to them. The abandonment of the true God for idols was accompanied by the rejection of morality for wickedness. As an act of judgement, God has at times handed over those who abandon him to their futile opinions and wicked ways (Rom. 1:18-32).

The Hindu, the Moslem, the animist, etc., are all testifying to their basic sense of a need for God and his law. Their error is in seeking false gods to meet their need. The religious and moral sensitivities of such people, although wickedly misdirected, testify to the basic nature of man.

Secondly, we need to note how the Scriptures view atheism. In the Old Testament the atheist is described as a 'fool' (Ps. 14:1). Now the Hebrew concept of a fool is not someone who is intellectually naïve, but a person who is stupid, impious, abandoned and wicked. The atheist's atheism is in the context of his moral corruption (Ps. 14). It is wickedness that makes men atheists, not superior intelligence or rational progress!

How is it possible for the Scriptures to link atheism with wickedness? Paul tells us that atheism and the abandonment of the true God are an impiety and unrighteousness against which the wrath of God is directed. They are a product of a resistance to the truth that God has made clear to men about his existence and character. No man can be an atheist without first rejecting God's self-revelation.

There is a dispute as to whether Paul says that men 'hold down' and suppress the truth, or 'hold back' and restrain it (Rom. 1:18). Scriptural parallels seem to favour the latter (2 Thess. 2:6-7; Luke 4:42; Philem. 13). However, this dispute does not affect the fact that God's self-revealing in creation (and in our religious and moral sense) has to be resisted before false gods, or no gods, may be followed. This resistance takes place in unrighteousness (Rom. 1:18). It is evil resistance of God and his revelation.

Neither atheism nor agnosticism is a neutral position. They are certainly not respectable. They are rebellious opinions held in defiance of God's self-revelation. As such they are entirely unnatural positions for humans to assert. Atheism may be learned, taught and adopted, but it cannot be neutral.

A simple illustration may help. Let us imagine you take a child to a city. You visit an art gallery. As the child looks at the paintings he asks numerous natural questions, including, 'Who painted that?' You move on to a science museum. Among his questions inevitably comes: 'Who invented that?' He is by nature a creationist. Paintings have painters; inventions have inventors. Which child (or adult) would *naturally* ask, 'By what process did that painting (or invention) evolve by chance?' The question would be treated with derision and the child told, 'Paintings and inventions do not just happen; people have to produce them.'

Cross the road to a natural history museum and a child (and adult) would *naturally* respond in the same way. He would see in God's handiwork God's imprint. He would look for a creator. How many parents have been asked by children, 'Who made the stars? Who made the grass?' However, a child (or adult) may be *taught* to restrain his natural questions and to ask, 'How many years ago did this evolve, and from what?' Atheism may be taught, but it is contrary to nature.

Conclusion

We began by asking why God's existence is presupposed in scriptural writings and scriptural preaching. The answer ought now to be clear. The biblical pattern is to presuppose the existence of God because God is constantly making himself and his will known to man through creation and his religious and moral sense.

We are not preaching to men who are naturally atheists, irreligious and amoral, but to men who, under all the veneer of godlessness, *know* there is a God and *know* they have responsibilities towards him and his creatures. Their vaunted atheism is sin against knowledge. It is not our job to accept that their rebelliousness is respectable, but to expose the shallowness and falseness of their assertion. They want us to relate to them in their wilful ignorance. Their knowledge of God and his will is under the surface of their professed atheism. A submarine may be forced to surface by a well-placed depth-charge. Similarly, an atheist may be forced to acknowledge the truth about God and his will, hidden deep in his heart, by a preacher's insistence that he *does* know what he denies. There is no escape from God.

Special revelation

To desire to know God without God is impossible; there is no knowledge without him who is the prime source of knowledge.
Frederick van Baader

There may be a theology without the Scriptures — a theology of nature, gathered by painful and slow, and sometimes doubtful processes from what a man sees around him and what he sees within him. In like manner there may be an astronomy of nature gathered by man's naked eye in the field at night. But what is this astronomy of nature to the astronomy of the telescope? The Word of God is to theology as, but vastly much more than, these instruments are to astronomy.
Benjamin Warfield

In the act of revelation, God is speaking, demonstrating, proving; man is hearing, learning, receiving.

J. J. Van Oosterzee

3.
Special revelation

We have asserted that God is constantly making himself and his will known to man through creation and his religious and moral sense. This leaves man inexcusable for atheism or agnosticism, but in possession of only a very limited knowledge of God. To know that God exists, that he is eternal and powerful, is worthy to be worshipped and is concerned with right and wrong, is important and foundational. It gives a creature knowledge of his Creator, but falls far short of what a *sinful* creature needs to know about God. To know enough to be rendered inexcusable for the misuse of the knowledge is not to know enough to be delivered from the consequences of that misuse. A general revelation suits creatures, but not sinners.

God, having determined to save people for himself from among those who have restrained their knowledge of him and pursued unrighteousness, has provided this additional knowledge. It has not, however, been given as a general revelation to all men, but to specific individuals. It has, therefore, been termed 'special revelation'.

This 'special revelation' has been granted in different forms through all ages. During the Old Testament era there were six main modes of revelation and during the New Testament era four. Each mode needs individual consideration.

The Old Testament

1. Theophany

The combination of the Greek words *'theos'* and *'phanein'*, meaning 'God' and 'to appear' respectively, define a theophany as 'an appearance of God'. The patriarchs especially were granted theophanies.

The most detailed account of a theophany is in Genesis 18. Moses explains that the LORD appeared to Abraham (v. 1) and that this appearance occurred in the visit of three 'men' (v. 2). One of these 'men' speaks as the LORD and makes specific promises to Abraham and Sarah (vv. 9-15). When they leave, Abraham walks with them (v. 16). The LORD continues a conversation with Abraham and then leaves him (v. 33). The other two men, now described as 'angels' (19:1), but still appearing to be men (19:5), go on to Sodom.

The fact that God is invisible and incorporeal in himself should not make us conclude that a theophany was a hallucination, or a vision. The God who created matter can surely take on a material form in order to converse with men. A temporary incarnation for God should be no problem to those who believe in the incarnation of Christ.

Indeed, it is arguable that the scriptural affirmations that no one has ever seen God other than as he is made known in Christ (John 1:18), that there is no more that man can know of God in this life other than as he is seen in Christ (John 14:8-9), and that Isaiah's vision of God was a vision of the glory of Christ (John 12:39-41) indicate that the pre-incarnation appearances of God were appearances of God the Son. The fact that Christ is the Word (John 1:1) and that the Old Testament prophets spoke according to the Spirit of Christ in them (1 Peter 1:11) also encourages this suggestion, although it should not be affirmed dogmatically as though it were unquestionably true.

2. The Angel of the LORD

Closely linked to theophanies and pre-incarnation appearances of Christ is that enigmatic being, the Angel of the LORD. There are over one hundred references to angels in the Old Testament, but among these are specific references to one angel called the Angel of the LORD.

This angel is distinguished from other angels because he speaks as God, delivering his message in the first person singular, and himself promises to fulfil his word (Gen. 16:10; 22:12). In delivering his message he is described variously as 'the Angel of the LORD' and 'the LORD' himself, suggesting an identification of the two (Judg. 6:11,12,14,16,18,20). Those to whom the Angel of the LORD appeared responded to him and worshipped him as God himself (Gen. 16:13-14; Judg. 6:24). Nor is there any hesitancy on the part of the Angel of the LORD in receiving worship that God alone should receive, a hesitancy elsewhere specifically recorded when mere angels are involved (Rev. 22:8-9).

It might, however, be objected that the angel spoke in the first person singular and was identified with God so closely only because as an ambassador of God he delivered his message in the place of God. Paul, as Christ's ambassador, could implore his readers on Christ's behalf (2 Cor. 5:20). There is a truth here, as far as it goes, but no one would argue that Paul identifies himself with God, or is identified by others with God, in quite the same way as the angel of the LORD is identified with the LORD.

In addition, we need to note that the LORD is sometimes specifically and explicitly identified with an angel. The parallelism used by Jacob and Malachi require that Jacob's God and his Angel are one and that Malachi's prophecy is fulfilled by the LORD, the Angel of the covenant (Gen. 48:15-16; Mal. 3:1). To try to make them two separate beings would be a great misunderstanding of the fundamental nature of parallelism in the writings of the Old Testament.

The same reasoning that suggested that the God revealed in theophany would be God the Son is applicable to God's self-revelation in the Angel of the LORD.

3. The audible voice

The rarest form of self-revelation used by God in the Old Testament was his voice. At Sinai, when he gave Israel the Ten Commandments, he adopted no form that they could see, but they heard him declare the Ten Commandments with his voice (Deut. 4:12-13,15). The lack of form was a deliberate discouragement to idolatry.

Moses recognized that to hear the voice of God was a unique and momentous experience, an amazing act of condescension that mortal men should hear the voice of God and live (Deut. 4:12-20,32-34). The effect on the Israelites was to fill them with sheer terror, so that they pleaded that God might accept Moses as a mediator through whom God should speak to them (Deut. 5:22-28). This pleading was heard and God's self-revelation was mediated through men throughout the remainder of the Old Testament era.

4. Urim and Thummim

One of the means by which Israel sought and obtained guidance from God from the time that a priesthood was established among them was by the use of the Urim and Thummim kept by the high priest (Exod. 28:30; Num. 27:21).

If it is correct to interpret the references in the historical books of the Old Testament to 'enquiring of the LORD' as indications of the use of the Urim and Thummim, then it is evident that positive, negative and non-committal answers could be received (1 Sam. 23:9-12; 1 Chron. 14:14; 1 Sam. 28:6).

The terms 'Urim and Thummim' literally mean 'lights' and 'perfections', but neither the significance of these names, nor the manner in which guidance was given, is now understood. Guesses abound but facts are short.

5. Moses

The importance of Moses in the Old Testament is not likely to be overstated. We have already noted how the Israelites asked that God would speak to them through him. Moses stands as the mediator of the Old Covenant in the same way as our Lord is the mediator of the New Covenant. Law came through Moses; grace and truth through Jesus Christ (John 1:17; 2 Cor. 3). Of course, there is a distinction: Moses is God's servant; Jesus is God's Son.

God did use other people, especially the prophets, to reveal his truth in the Old Testament era but, as Aaron and Miriam found to their cost, when they insisted on equality with Moses because God had also spoken through them, God himself put a distinction between Moses and all other prophets (Num. 12:1-8).

Whereas God revealed himself and his truth to his prophets in dreams and visions, Moses was given three distinct and distinguishing privileges:

1. God spoke with him 'face to face' (literally 'mouth to mouth').
2. God spoke 'clearly and not in riddles'.
3. Moses saw 'the form of the LORD'

(Num. 12:8).

The phrase 'face to face', or 'mouth to mouth', does not denote some special intimacy between close friends. It emphasizes personal contact, as opposed to impersonal contact (cf. Deut. 34:10; Jer. 32:4; 2 John 12; 3 John 14). God spoke to the prophets in dreams and visions. His message was mediated through those means. To Moses, however, he spoke personally and directly.

The messages conveyed to the prophets are full of symbols, enigmas and puzzles. Anyone in doubt should read Ezekiel! God spoke to Moses, however, clearly in straightforward prose. It was not unusual for the Old Testament prophets to be puzzled by the things they saw and heard (1 Peter 1:10-12; Dan. 12:8-9), but Moses was given a clear grasp of the truth.

The prophets' contact with God was mainly through dreams and visions, but Moses continued to be granted theophanies. At Sinai the Israelites had heard a voice but had seen no form. Moses was granted a voice and a form with whom to speak.

Of course, it needs to be underlined that to see the form of God in a theophany is not the same as seeing God as he really is. Even at his highest experience of communion with God, Moses could only see his 'back' and not his 'face' (Exod. 33:18-23). Although Moses had higher privileges of communion with God than anyone else in the Old Testament, his experience of God is far below our Lord's (John 1:18).

6. The prophets

Next to Moses, no group of people was more important as recipients of revelation than the Old Testament prophets. The titles given to them reveal something of their function.

A prophet could be described as a 'man of God' (1 Kings 13:1), not simply because he was devoted to the service of God, but because he 'spoke from God'. His prophecy did not originate from his own mind. He was not a commentator looking at life and seeking to unravel its mysteries. Peter uses a term which means to 'loosen' and states that scriptural prophecies were not a product of the prophet's own attempts to untie life's 'knots' (2 Peter 1:20-21). He was not a puzzle-solver, but a man with a message that had come from God.

Prophets were also described as 'seers' because of their special insight and the fact that they usually received their messages from God by seeing dreams and visions (1 Sam. 9:3-9; 2 Sam. 15:27). The messages that came from God were presented by God to their eyes and ears (Num. 12:6). Even the false prophets understood that they had to claim dreams and visions if their credibility as prophets was to be considered seriously (Jer. 23:16-32).

The term 'prophet' itself alludes to the prophet as a spokesman. When the LORD reassured Moses that he had made him as God to Pharaoh, and that Aaron would be Moses' prophet (Exod. 7:1), he explained it to mean that Aaron would speak for Moses as if he were Moses' mouth and Moses would be as God to Aaron, putting words in his mouth (Exod. 4:15-16). The prophet is a person who has words put in his mouth and acts as God's mouthpiece. He speaks God's words as God's mouth. Essential to all prophecy is the idea of speech that is inspired by God.

Prophecy usually occurred in three stages:

1. It originated with God as his message.
2. It was transmitted by God through dreams and visions to his messenger.
3. It was communicated by the prophet to the hearers.

The question might arise as to whether the message changes at all in any of these stages. Is it corrupted to any degree? Peter asserts that the prophecy originates with God, not the prophet, and that when the prophet speaks, he speaks 'from God' and does so being 'carried along by the Holy Spirit' (2 Peter 1:20-21). He speaks not as a free agent, but under the Holy Spirit's direction. A person who is being carried along is in the power of the carrier. He goes where he is taken. The prophet speaks as one who is under the authority of another.

It might be argued that a true prophet (i.e. one whose message is from God and is not his own production) might be tempted to change the message and so corrupt it. The case of Balaam demonstrates that this was not possible.

There is no doubt that Balaam was a very wicked man and would do anything to gain money. The Israelites had no hesitation in executing him for teaching the Midianites how to lead Israel into sin (Num. 31:8), and he is viewed in Scripture as an evil man (2 Peter 2:15-16; Jude 11; Rev. 2:14). Nevertheless, Balaam was a prophet.

Balak, King of Moab, offered Balaam great financial reward if he would curse Israel (Num. 22-24). There is no doubt that Balaam wanted the reward. He tried in many ways to gain it. However, throughout his dealings with Balak, Balaam insisted that he could only prophesy when the Lord allowed him to and he could only say what God put in his mouth (Num. 22:13,18-19,38; 23:3,12,26; 24:12-14). To prophesy anything other than the Word of God under inspiration was *impossible*. The integrity of the message was divinely assured.

The close of the Old Testament revelation

The revelation that God gave to Israel from the days of the patriarchs through to the restoration from the exile was viewed by the Jews as having ceased with the prophetic ministry of Malachi. So decisive was this cessation that the rabbis expressed it as the departure of the Holy Spirit from Israel.

In the inter-testamental period Jewish writers lamented, 'At this time there is no prince, or prophet, or leader, no burnt offering, or sacrifice,' and 'The prophets have fallen asleep.'[1]

A time of great disaster was described in 1 Maccabees as unparalleled 'since the time that prophets ceased to appear among them'. Both the Jews living in Israel and those co-cooned in the Qumran community made temporary decisions until a prophet would come to tell them what to do.[2]

The cessation of the ministry of prophets and the expectation of future prophets meant that inter-testamental Judaism could not find the authoritative voice of God in living prophets. However, Malachi had shown Israel her duty. His final words, 'Remember the law of ... Moses' (Mal. 4:4), pointed her to the written Word rather than the spoken prophecy, and emphasized the need for the understanding and practice of the law.

During the inter-testamental period the prophets no longer prophesied but the Old Testament Scriptures themselves became Israel's prophets. Between the days of Malachi, the final Jewish prophet, and the days of the Elijah whose coming was foretold by Malachi and whom our Lord identified as John the Baptist, 'All the Prophets and the Law prophesied' (Mal. 4:5-6; Matt. 11:13,14). The Word of God no longer came through a human voice but in the written Word.

The New Testament

1. John the Baptist

Malachi's closing promise that God would send the prophet Elijah before he sent judgement, to bring about a change of heart in the people (Mal. 4:5-6), was unfulfilled for some 450 years. However, the announcement of the birth of John to his father Zechariah promised that he would fulfil Malachi's prophecy, not as a literal Elijah returned from heaven, but in the spirit and power of Elijah (Luke 1:17).

The inter-testamental period, devoid of living prophets, ended when the word of the Lord came to John and he began his preaching ministry (Luke 3:2-3). John had no hesitation in denying that he was literally Elijah, a typical literalistic interpretation of Malachi popular with the Jews (John 1:21). Jesus had no doubt that John was the Elijah Malachi had promised and that his ministry ended the Old Testament era and commenced the Messianic era of the kingdom of God (Matt. 11:7-15).

John's role as 'Elijah' was to be a forerunner, a herald preparing the way for the Lord himself by requiring his hearers to repent in preparation for the arrival of the King, Jesus himself (John 1:23,29-31). He had responsibilities similar to those of a best man at a wedding, but was not himself the focus of attention. He had to diminish in the public view as our Lord increased (John 3:28-30).

2. The Lord Jesus Christ

The role of the Lord Jesus Christ in special revelation is unique. This uniqueness arises from his person — who he is. God gave to his Old Testament messengers honoured titles befitting their role. He spoke of 'my servants the prophets' (Zech. 1:6) and exalted Moses above them as a servant 'faithful in all his house'. Jesus, however, was no mere servant, nor merely in God's house, but a Son over God's house (Heb. 1:1,2; 3:1-6).

To his prophets God had revealed himself in dreams and visions, but to Moses in a voice and a form (Num. 12:6-8). None of these, however, had ever seen God as he is, but Jesus,

God's Son, had come from God to make him known as only a Son could reveal his Father, out of a relationship of unique and intimate knowledge (John 1:18; Matt. 11:27).

Our Lord's revelation of God was not, however, simply in words but in everything he was. Consequently, he is 'the Word', the message of God to man, the explanation of the divine mind (John 1:1,14). He is the 'the truth', revealing a message from God in his teaching, but also in his character, so that to have seen him is to have seen all that can be known of God in this world (John 14:6-11).

All the special revelation of God centres in him. The Old Testament revelation given through the prophets was inspired by the Spirit of Christ in them (1 Peter 1:11). No dichotomy may be drawn between the 'primitive' ideas of the Old Testament and the more 'enlightened' teaching of Jesus. The message of the prophets was inspired by Jesus. Hence his ability to explain why Moses had to make concessions to human sinfulness in framing the divorce law contrary to the spirit of the creation ordinance of marriage (Matt. 19:3-9). From this arises his dismissal of the traditional interpretation of the law and the restoration of its true meaning (Matt. 5:17-48). The inspirer of Old Testament revelation is its perfect expositor.

In the same way, the revelation given to the apostles is not an addendum to, or development of, his teaching. We may not set the 'original' teaching of Jesus over against its 'development' by his apostles. Rather, he promised those apostles that the Spirit would guide them into all truth when he took what belonged to Christ and made it known to them (John 16:12-15). The truth taught by the Spirit to the apostles is Christ's truth. The Old Testament prophets and New Testament apostles spoke the truth of Christ. All special revelation meets in him and is issued by his inspiration with his imprimatur.

3. The apostles

Christ's apostles had to have four qualifications. Firstly, they were appointed by the Lord Jesus Christ himself (Mark 3:14; Acts 1:24; Gal. 1:1). Secondly, they had to have the proven ability to do miracles (Matt. 10:8; 2 Cor. 12:12). Thirdly, they had to be witnesses to the resurrection of Christ (Acts 1:22; 1 Cor. 9:1) and, fourthly, they had to be recipients of revelation (Gal. 1:11-12; Eph. 3:5).

We have already seen that the revelation which the apostles received was granted to them by Christ through the Holy Spirit. He entrusted them with his truth. The Spirit of God gave the apostles accurate memory of the teaching that Jesus had given on earth and taught them all truth. It was 'all truth' because it was all that Jesus wanted them to know which they had not been capable of receiving during his earthly ministry (John 15:26; 16:12-15).

Their responsibility as custodians of the truth was to pass on to others what they had received from the Lord so that their hearers might hold on to those teachings without amendment (1 Cor. 11:2,23; 15:3; 2 Thess. 2:15; 2 Tim. 1:13). As with the Old Testament prophets, they were neither creators nor developers of the truth revealed, but proclaimers. For this reason their teachings, whether spoken or written, were to be received as from Christ himself. To agree with the apostles was to be in harmony with God. To disagree with the apostles was to be in a state of alienation from God (1 Cor. 14:37-38; 1 John 4:5-6).

4. The prophets

Alongside the limited number of New Testament apostles were a larger number of New Testament prophets. Whereas the ministry of John the Baptist marked the inauguration of the

Messianic age, during which salvation was accomplished for the church through the life and death of the Messiah, the exaltation and glorification of the Christ were marked by the outpouring of the Holy Spirit (Acts 2:22-36), so that the salvation which had been accomplished might be applied.

The Old Testament prophet Joel had prophesied that in the last days, the days of the Messiah, the Spirit of God would be poured out on all people. This age of the Spirit would culminate in the great and glorious Day of the Lord, which itself would be preceded by immense and universal upheavals. Yet the period between the outpouring of the Spirit and the Day of the Lord would be a day of salvation for those who called on the name of the Lord. This age of the Spirit would begin with a new era of dreams and visions and prophecies (Joel 2:28-32).

The apostle Peter declared that Joel's prophecy was explicitly fulfilled on the Day of Pentecost (Acts 2:16-21). The essential element of all true prophecy was present — speech inspired by God. The disciples spoke as the Spirit enabled them (Acts 2:4). On this occasion, however, there was an added element. They declared the wonders of God, by the enabling of the Spirit, in languages they had not learned (Acts 2:9-11).

Speaking in unlearned languages, or 'tongues', was not a mindless activity, a babble of meaningless vocal noise. It was a declaration of 'mysteries' in an unlearned language (1 Cor. 14:2). The term 'mystery' in the New Testament does not mean a problem difficult to understand. It is a technical term denoting a truth that has been made known by revelation (Rom. 16:25; 1 Cor. 15:51; Eph. 5:32). It was because tongues involved revelation that, when interpreted, they were equivalent to prophecy (1 Cor. 14:5).

New Testament prophecy is described as the receiving of revelation and the person who prophesies is referred to as a prophet (1 Cor. 14:30-31,37). The apostles and prophets of

the New Testament era are partakers of the same revelation of
the mystery of Christ revealed by the Spirit (Eph. 3:4-5).

What is the difference between an apostle and a prophet in
the New Testament? We have seen that apostles had to have
four qualifications. These made them unique witnesses to
Christ's resurrection and gave them a lifelong and church-wide
authority over life and doctrine, whereas prophets were simply the occasional organs of inspiration. The man to whom
truth was revealed occasionally was expected to be submis-
sive to the men to whom God had revealed *all* truth.

Conclusion

In these ten ways God revealed himself over some thousands
of years. However, because it was special revelation, and not
given to all men, it was necessary that a record of that revelation should be made. It is precisely this record that the Holy
Scriptures claim to be. Revelation is preserved to us in the
written Word of God.

Canonical Scripture
and its authority

The Old Testament canon (i.e. the thirty-nine books of the first-century Palestinian canon, Jesus' Bible) came to the church from the hands, as it were, of Christ and his apostles, from whom Christianity's credentials presupposed the divine authority of the Jewish Scriptures which the Christian facts fulfilled.

J. I. Packer

The principle of canonicity was not apostolic authorship but imposition by the apostles as 'law'.

Benjamin Warfield

It is God's voice, not man's; the words are God's words, the words of the Eternal, the Invisible, the Almighty, the Jehovah of this earth. The Bible is God's Bible; and when I see it I seem to hear a voice springing up from it saying, 'I am the book of God; man, read me. I am God's writing.'

C. H. Spurgeon

4.
Canonical Scripture and its authority

God's general revelation to all men[1] has been supplemented by a special revelation to specific men given in two stages: the Old Testament era and the New Testament era.[2] The fact that specific men received this revelation makes it liable to be lost to the rest of humanity unless the content of that revelation is recorded.

Writing is known to have been well advanced from before 3000 B.C. in the Ancient Near East and, therefore, to have been a part of society even in pre-patriarchal days. When we read of Moses being commanded to write God's judgement against Amalek on a scroll (Exod. 17:14-16), he would have had no difficulty in fulfilling the command.

Throughout the books which constitute our Old Testament there are many references to obeying laws written in books, placing a high esteem on written laws and studying books (e.g. Josh. 1:7-8; 1 Kings 2:3; Ps. 119; Dan. 9:2).

Which books are a record of special revelation in the Old Testament era?

We shall seek to answer this question from two perspectives: first, that of the Jews and, second, that of Christ and his apostles. Then, thirdly, we shall seek to answer one objection based on references to non-canonical books.

1. The Jews

We have seen in earlier chapters that the Jews who lived after the days of Malachi, in the centuries leading up to the coming of Christ and as contemporaries of Christ and his apostles, saw the days of Haggai, Zechariah and Malachi as the end of the age of the prophets. They looked forward to the days when Messiah would come, but saw no real prophets existing in their own days. As the rabbis expressed it so dramatically, 'The Holy Spirit had departed from Israel.'[3]

The Jews also accepted that throughout the age of the prophets, and dating back to the days of Moses, there had been a constant succession of prophets. These prophets had not only spoken under inspiration, but they also wrote, as Josephus expressed it, 'as they were taught by the very inspiration of God... Prophets have written the original and earliest account of things as they learned them of God himself by inspiration.'[4] The prophets were God's mouth and God's hand, his mouthpieces and his penmen.

Once the succession of prophets ceased, not only did verbal prophecy cease, but no more prophetic Scriptures could be written. All the writings subsequent to the days of the prophets were 'not worthy of equal credit with the earlier records because there has not been since the exact succession of prophets'.[5]

The Jews considered the Old Testament canon as containing either twenty-four or twenty-two books. The difference in number is simply due to the tendency to treat Judges and Ruth as either one book or two and to treat Jeremiah and Lamentations in the same way. These twenty-two or twenty-four books are parallel to our thirty-nine books, but are computed differently — e.g. the twelve minor prophets are considered as one book, not twelve. The books begin with Genesis and end with Chronicles.

There is evidence as early as the second century B.C. for the division of the Old Testament into three sections.[6] (The order of books in our Bible is different from the order of the Hebrew Bible. Our order owes more to the Greek Bible, the Septuagint, than to the Hebrew.) These three sections were the Law, the Prophets and the Writings.

When Jeshua Ben Sira translated his grandfather's book 'Ecclesiasticus' into Greek in 132 B.C., he described his relative in the preface as a student of 'the law and the prophets and the other books of the fathers' and 'the law itself, the prophecies and the rest of the books'.[7]

Philo of Alexandria (*c.* 20 B.C. - A.D. 50) also indicates a threefold division of the canon, referring to 'the laws, inspired oracles given through the prophets, hymns and the other books by which knowledge and piety may be increased and brought to perfection'.[8]

Among some Jews the Old Testament was also referred to under the dual heading of 'the Law and the Prophets'. This title appears in the apocryphal book 2 Maccabees and is found within four references in documents discovered from Qumran.[9]

It is, therefore, clear that the various Jewish sects of the Christian era had no substantial differences over the limits of canonical Scripture. Pharisees, Sadducees and Essenes accepted the same body of authoritative literature as the authentic, inspired record of God's revelation to Israel.

2. The view of Christ and his apostles

It has been confidently asserted that 'Our Lord and his apostles might differ from the religious leaders of Israel about the meaning of the Scriptures; there is no suggestion that they differed about the limits of the Scriptures,' and that 'When we think of Jesus and his Palestinian apostles we may be confident that they agreed with contemporary leaders in Israel about the contents of the canon.'[10]

Support for these assertions comes from the New Testament. There are numerous quotations from, and allusions to, the Old Testament throughout the New Testament writings. One study lists nearly 150 such quotations and allusions in the sayings of Jesus in the first three Gospels alone.[11] Another claims that 10% of all the recorded words of Jesus were quotations from the Old Testament.[12] At the back of my Greek New Testament there is a list of over 350 quotations from the Old Testament found in the New Testament, from Matthew to 2 Peter.[13] Our Lord and his apostles saturated their writings and sayings with the Old Testament.

Whenever our Lord deviated from the Pharisees about 'Scripture', the debate was never over which books constituted Scripture, but always over the interpretation of Scripture. When the Lord referred to 'the Law', or 'the Law and the Prophets' or 'the Law, the Prophets and the Psalms', no one ever asked him to define what he meant (see John 10:32-34; Matt. 5:17; Luke 24:44-45). There was an agreement on the canon of Old Testament Scripture. No Jew would have misunderstood our Lord's spoken warning that all the righteous blood shed from the days of Abel to Zechariah, son of Berakiah, would be visited on that generation (Matt. 23:35-36). Abel's murder was recorded in Genesis (Gen. 4:8), the first book of the Hebrew Old Testament; Zechariah's murder is reported in Chronicles (2 Chron. 24:20-22), the last book of the Hebrew Old Testament. Jesus was warning that all the guilt that had been incurred from the first to the last page of Old Testament Scripture would be visited on them. By so saying, he indicated his acceptance of the limits of the Hebrew canon.

3. The New Testament use of apocryphal books

A challenge has been raised to the claim that our Lord and his apostles only held Old Testament books to be canonical on the grounds that in the New Testament there are allusions to, and quotations from, non-canonical sources.

Dennefield saw a reference in our Lord's command that we should forgive men when they sin against us, so that God might forgive us our sins (Matt. 6:14), to the apocryphal statement: 'Forgive your neighbour the hurt that he has done you and then your sins will be pardoned when you pray' (Ecclesiasticus 28:2).[14] He found half a dozen similar parallels.

However, the existence of parallels between biblical and non-biblical literature should not surprise us. To find parallel ideas in non-canonical books does not imply any necessary dependence, nor does it make a book canonical because on one issue it expresses a truth. Throughout Christian history there have been those who have had a high regard for the Greek philosopher Plato and found 'Christian' ideas in his writings, but no one now seriously suggests that Jesus made allusions to the writings of Plato, or considered his works canonical.

Emphasis has sometimes also been placed on the acceptance by biblical writers of ideas from non-canonical sources — e.g. Paul names the Egyptian magicians who opposed Moses as Jannes and Jambres (2 Tim. 3:8), names not mentioned in the Old Testament, but frequently mentioned in Jewish tradition. Jude alludes to a dispute over Moses' body (Jude 9); again this is not recorded in the Old Testament, but is reported in Jewish tradition.

It cannot, however, be argued that the acceptance of a particular fact from a traditional source gives credence to the whole tradition, or canonizes the whole source. To appeal to something because it is true in one respect does not require it to be treated as true in all respects.

Special emphasis is placed on Jude's reference to Enoch's prophecy (Jude 14-15). It is argued that a quotation from an extra-canonical source implies the acceptance of the source as canonical. The fallacy of this reasoning is evident as soon as that principle is applied to Paul's quotations from heathen poets such as Epimenides, Aratus and Menander (Acts 17:28; 1 Cor. 15:33; Titus 1:12). There is a difference between quoting a source and quoting a source *as Scripture*. Many truthful things have been written outside of the Bible and not all truth is biblical.

Allusions and quotations occur in Scripture to writings which are truthful in regard to the thing quoted. The Scriptures themselves are quoted because as a whole they were considered truthful by Jesus and his apostles and the Jews of their day.

What degree of authority did the canonical books have?

We shall again seek to understand, first, the Jewish view and, second, the view of Christ and his apostles.

1. The Jewish view

Philo the Alexandrian expressed the view of Scripture held by every loyal Jew in the inter-testamental age and the first century A.D. when he said, 'The Jews would die 10,000 times rather than to permit one single word to be altered of their Scriptures.'[15]

Josephus also reflected the same commitment to the harmony and authority of the canonical Scriptures, tracing their authority and accuracy to their divine inspiration: 'Nothing can be better attested than the writings authorized among us. In fact, they could not be subject to any discord, for only that which the prophets wrote ages ago is approved among us, as they were taught by the very inspiration of God... For we have not an innumerable multitude of books among us, disagreeing from and contradicting one another, but only twenty-two books, which contain the records of all past times; which are justly believed to be divine... During so many ages as have already passed, no one has been so bold as either to add anything to them, to take anything from them, or to make any change in them; but it is become natural to all Jews ... to esteem these books to contain divine doctrines, and to persist in them and, if occasion be, willingly to die for them... Prophets have written the original and earliest accounts of things as they learned them of God himself by inspiration.'[16]

The great authority on Judaism G. F. Moore summarized the Jewish attitude as follows: 'It was an uncontested axiom that every syllable of Scripture had the veracity and authority of the Word of God.'[17]

2. The view of Christ and his apostles

Did Jesus and his apostles also view the Old Testament as 'inspired of God', 'divine', 'not subject to any discord' and as 'the Word of God' in 'every syllable'? We have already noted the extensive use of the Old Testament in the New Testament writings and that the doctrines and opinions of the Old Testament are widely quoted and allusions are frequently made to them.

Specific statements

There are, however, in addition specific statements about the authority and inspiration of Old Testament Scripture. We shall consider one from our Lord and the other from Paul.

In a dispute over his right to refer to himself as the Son of God, our Lord quoted Psalm 82 and supported its authority by the affirmation: 'And the Scripture cannot be broken' (John

10:35). The verb 'broken' has the meaning of 'rendered void' or 'invalidated'. It is a clear statement of our Lord's view of Scripture and its unbreakable authority. In making a statement, almost casually in the middle of a debate, he demonstrated how fundamental this way of thinking about Scripture was to him. He and his opponents were at least one in this view of scriptural authority. As C. K. Barrett comments, 'The principle was an axiom both to Judaism and primitive Christianity: the two differed only in their beliefs about the fulfilment of Scripture.'[18]

When we turn to Paul we have in 2 Timothy 3:16 the clear statement that 'All Scripture is God-breathed' (Greek, *theopneustos*). B. B. Warfield long ago demonstrated by reference to parallel words consisting of *theos*, a verb and the ending '*-tos*', that the meaning is passive.[19] The Scriptures do not breathe out God; God breathes out Scripture. The Scriptures, the writings themselves, are his Word, proceeding from his mouth.

The harmony of Paul's view with the Jewish view of his day can be seen by comparing his statement with that of Josephus, who claimed that the Old Testament prophets wrote the Scriptures 'according to the *"pneustia"*: that which originates in God'.[20]

Specific attitudes

We are not, however, merely left to specific statements, but to specific attitudes to Scripture which show the general view that Christ and his apostles had of Scripture.

For our Lord and his apostles, whatever the Scriptures said had the authority of God himself. The Old Testament Scriptures record the institution and definition of marriage without identifying the speaker (Gen. 2:24). The New Testament attributes the words to the Creator himself (Matt. 19:4-5). The second psalm lacks any introduction in the Psalter, but its words are recorded in the New Testament as God speaking through the Holy Spirit by the mouth of David (Acts 4:25).The first chapter of Hebrews is full of Old Testament quotations which are unattributed there but attributed to God in the New (cf. Deut. 32:43 with Heb. 1:6; Ps. 45:6-7 with Heb. 1:8-9; Ps. 102:25-27 with Heb. 1:10-12). It is evident that the New Testament identifies what Scripture says with what God says.

In addition to this, there are many examples of arguments that hinge upon the minutest details of the Old Testament. This is not surprising, as Jesus gave authority to the smallest letter and least stroke of a pen in the Old Testament (Matt. 5:18).

In the New Testament arguments could be based on single words used in the Old Testament. Our Lord built arguments on the Old Testament use of the words 'lord' and 'gods' (Matt. 22:45; John 10:34). The writer of the epistle to the Hebrews argues on the basis of the words 'today' and 'rest', as well as the phrase 'yet once more' (Heb. 3:7-11; 12:26).

Even more powerfully, the New Testament Scriptures build arguments on verb tenses, singular and plural forms of nouns and Old Testament silences. Our Lord proved the resurrection from the fact that God said, 'I *am*,' not 'I was' or 'I will be' (Matt. 22:32). Paul argued for the significance of 'seed', not 'seeds' (Gal. 3:16). Melchizedek's history is drawn from Old Testament omissions (Heb. 7:3).

Argument at this level, with this degree of confidence in the detail of the Old Testament, demonstrates the reliability that the Lord and his apostles considered the Old Testament to have. To them it was infallible (trustworthy) and inerrant (free from error). Coming from God's mouth, it could not be rendered false.

Is the Christian canon wider than the Jewish?

1. The New Testament evidence

In considering special revelation we saw that a new age of revelation dawned with John the Baptist. Our Lord and his apostles revealed the truth that belonged to Christ.

Our Lord was entirely confident that none of his words would be lost and gave the Holy Spirit to his apostles to ensure their perfect memory of his teaching, as well as to guide them into all truth (Matt. 24:35; John 14:26; 16:13).

The apostles fulfilled their responsibility not only by teaching but also by writing. The false teachers soon understood this and from the beginning began to forge letters as if from the apostles. The apostles had to take care to maintain the authority of all their own teachings, whether given by letter or by word of mouth, as well as to distinguish them from forgeries by various means (2 Thess. 2:2,15; 3:17; Gal. 6:11).

When the apostles wrote their letters they were conscious of possessing great authority. They commanded that their letters should be read to all the Christians (1 Thess. 5:27). They considered it the duty of all their readers to hold fast to the truths they had written and commanded separation from those who would not obey the command given in their letters (2 Thess. 2:15; 3:14-15).

This claim for authority did not arise merely out of their being recipients of revelation, but was accompanied by a conviction about their own inspiration as writers. They claimed to speak words not taught by human wisdom but taught by the Spirit and to be writing the Lord's commands (1 Cor. 2:13; 14:37).

Within the New Testament writings there is a recognition of each other's writings as Scripture. Therefore, Paul quotes both Deuteronomy 25:4 and Luke 10:7 verbatim after the introductory formula: 'The Scripture says...' (1 Tim. 5:18). It is entirely inadequate to argue that Paul was merely quoting a saying of Jesus, or even a collection of sayings, for neither of these could accurately be termed 'Scripture', a term used in the Bible for written canonical statements.

Peter also used the term 'Scripture' to describe New Testament writings. He reminds his readers that the teaching he was giving was consistent with the things 'our beloved Paul wrote according to the wisdom given him, as also in all his letters speaking in them concerning these things'. For Peter, Paul wrote according to the wisdom given to him. More than that, however, he warns them of the difficult things in Paul's letters which are easily twisted by unstable people who distort the writings of Paul, 'even as the rest of the Scriptures' (2 Peter 3:15-16). Peter has no hesitation in including Paul's letters in the Scriptures.

The apostle John also gave the Christians a test of orthodoxy. Whoever agreed with the apostles in their teaching was of God; whoever disagreed was not of God (1 John 4:1-6). All doctrine had to be tested by the standard of apostolic teaching, whether verbal or written.

2. The post-apostolic age

In the generations immediately following the apostolic age there were two sources of authority for the primitive church — the Old Testament and the apostolic testimony. In his study of early Christian doctrine, J. N. Kelly concludes that 'This two-fold appeal to the united witness of the Old Testament and the apostles was characteristic of the age.'[21]

For the church immediately after the apostles, 'The importance of the Old Testament as a doctrinal norm in the primitive

Church cannot be exaggerated... The parallel doctrinal norm, the testimony of the apostles, was equally important in theory, and of course more important in fact.'[22]

Faithfulness to the apostolic testimony meant that careful enquiries were made of those who had heard and been taught by the apostles as to their teaching, and this oral tradition was supplemented by an intense interest in the apostolic writings. Kelly affirms 'the high prestige enjoyed by the Pauline Epistles and the Gospels' and that 'The number of citations from them in this period is quite remarkable.' He goes on to assert that 'There is no evidence for beliefs or practices current in the period which were not vouched for in books later known as the New Testament.'[23]

The epistles of Paul began to be circulated as a group rather than as individual letters early on in the second century. The four Gospels as a collection followed soon after. The gathering of New Testament documents began soon after the close of the apostolic age.

3. The tests of canonicity

What did the early Christians require of a book before it was acknowledged as part of New Testament Scripture? The fundamental requirement was divine inspiration. If a book was to be given equal authority with the God-breathed writings of the Old Testament, it had to be God-breathed. How was inspiration to be tested?

The first question asked of a book was whether it had apostolic authorship. Those books which did have apostolic authority were readily accepted. Paul's epistles were, therefore, quickly received as inspired.

However, even at an early period, 'Apostolic authorship in the direct sense was not insisted on, if some form of apostolic authority could be established.'[24] Therefore, works by associates of the apostles and members of our Lord's family were also accepted because they had apostolic authorization. Paul's quotation of Luke in his first letter to Timothy authorized Luke's Gospel because it was recognized by an apostle as Scripture.

Additional to apostolic authorship or authorization was antiquity. Documents which post-dated the apostolic age could not be accepted as part of Scripture, however beneficial or orthodox their sentiments.

As increasing numbers of writings claiming to be apostolic arose in the second half of the second century, two other tests were used. These writings were scrutinized for anything unorthodox which would exclude them from being part of the truth and they were dismissed if they were only favoured by one party within Christendom rather than being widely accepted throughout the Christian world.

The fundamental reason for formally accepting a book as part of the New Testament was the divine inspiration given to its writing, which inspiration was communicated through, or accredited by, an apostle. As the Jews accepted the prophetic word from God, so the Christians accepted the apostolic word. Neither *made* a book part of Scripture. They simply *recognized* it as such.

Attitudes to Scripture

[Those who want us to turn] away from proper deference to God's words would have us instead make a basic commitment to the truth of some other words — our own perhaps, or those of scientists, or those of theologians.

John Frame

The question about the inspiration of Scripture really boils down to Christology. It is impossible to affirm his authority while at the same time seeking to evade his teaching regarding the divine authority of the Bible.

Clark Pinnock

[The Bible is] a vein of pure gold, unalloyed by quartz or any earthly substance. This is a star without a speck; a sun without a blot; a light without darkness; a moon without its paleness; a glory without a dimness. O Bible! It cannot be said of any other book that it is perfect and pure; but of thee we can declare all wisdom is gathered up in thee without a particle of folly.

Charles Spurgeon

5.
Attitudes to Scripture

We have seen that our Lord and his apostles shared a common attitude to the Scriptures with the Jews of their day. They believed the Scriptures to be the inspired Word of God, accurate and authoritative in all its parts and as a whole.

In the centuries following the apostolic age the churches generally held the same view of Scripture. It is widely accepted, even in secular circles, that 'The traditional view of the Bible is that it was *all* written under the guidance of God and that it is, therefore, *all* true.'[1]

Attacks on the traditional view of Scripture have gained momentum since the middle of the nineteenth century. Before then the Scriptures had been attacked by opponents outside the church, but only in the nineteenth century did attacks on the traditional doctrine from within the church begin in earnest.

We shall consider just five of the many attacks on the traditional attitude to Scripture which are current in our day.

1. The incarnation of Christ and scriptural authority

The implications of Christ's incarnation have often been debated. Particularly significant is our understanding of the nature of his 'emptying himself' (see Phil. 2:7). Does this imply a laying aside of deity itself, or a loss of the glorious position of exaltation that belongs to deity?

Historically, and I believe correctly, Christians have seen the 'emptying' in terms of a change of status, not of being. This traditional view is supported by the context of Philippians 2, where Christians are being called to follow an example of humility, by parallel passages (such as John 17:5; 2 Cor. 8:9) and by the fact that a change in God's being would be a declaration of his not being God because it would be a denial of his immutability.

However, those who support the view that Christ did cease to be God at his incarnation have sometimes added to it the idea that in taking on the likeness of sinful flesh (Rom. 8:3), he took on a body and mind that not only could experience the trials of this world, but were also limited to the viewpoints and perspectives of this world. Hence, it is argued that Christ became one of the people of his day and therefore adopted their views, including their view of the Old Testament. This is seen as a great act of condescension and humiliation on the part of the divine Logos.

The consequences of such a view of Christ are clear. He becomes culturally bound in his teaching and expresses himself in accordance with the ignorance and prejudices of his day. The position of modern man is exalted. He is not bound to accept the views of Christ any longer, for they are outdated, and he becomes the ultimate authority in deciding what Christ meant and how his teaching is applicable in the modern world after it has been 'demythologized'.

Such a view of the consequences of the incarnation is inconsistent with the biblical data. Christ claimed that his teaching was not his own, nor of this world. It had been given him by his Father and proceeded from a position of knowledge of heavenly realities (John 3:10-13; 6:38,63; 12:47-50; 14:6;

17:8,14). He claimed to be the *truth*, whose words would remain for ever, not a temporary teacher of passing views (Matt. 24:35). The apostles drew a distinction between the truth they taught, which was from God, and those who taught from this world's viewpoint (1 John 4:1-6).

An acceptance of Christ as merely 'a man of his day' would reduce his teaching to nothing more than of antiquarian interest and would be destructive of the idea that Christ taught truth of abiding value and continuing relevance. Such a view of Christ, far from showing the humility of God, merely makes his revelation in Christ irrelevant.

2. The humility of God and Scripture

The cry of 'Bibliolatry' is often raised against the traditional view of Scripture, and it is emphasized that religious authority is neither to be sought in the church nor the written word. Where, then, is it to be sought? To some authority rests in Christ himself, but they have difficulty in accepting the authority of Christ while rejecting his view of Scripture. Others say that the true authority in religion is God himself, and this is ultimately true, but what does it mean?

Often emphasis is put on 'encounter with God'. The more man-centred theologies speak of the need for man to seek encounter with God, and those which emphasize divine initiative focus on God's quest for man. Either way, authoritative and meaningful experience of God is not mediated through a book such as the Bible but in experiences of various sorts. To have an authentic and meaningful experience of God is the be-all and end-all of human existence.

In such theology the inspiration or accuracy of the Bible is an irrelevance. God may use it as part of his method of making himself known in encounter, but the significant part of the experience of God is not the means used, but the experience known.

Sometimes it is viewed as part of the great condescension of God that he deigns to use something so 'obviously human and flawed' as Scripture. Its 'mistakes' are said to emphasize the humility and skill of God in using such inadequate tools to break into the human soul.

No one expresses this view with more ability than Karl Barth: 'If God has not been ashamed to speak through the Scriptures with its fallible human words, with its historical and scientific blunders, its theological contradictions, with the uncertainty of its transmission and above all with its Jewish character, but rather accepted it in all its fallibility to make it serve him, we ought not to be ashamed of it when with all its fallibility it wants anew to be to us a witness.'[2]

What a contrast there is between Barth's attitude to Scripture and that of our Lord and his apostles! On only one point do they agree: that Scripture is a witness to God. In every other respect they are in total disagreement. Barth sees the Bible as full of fallible words; Christ argued on the basis of those words. Barth accepts that the Bible has historical, scientific and theological blunders; Christ quotes its historical and scientific passages with total confidence and finds no contradictions. Barth has problems with uncertain transmission; Christ is confident that it has been preserved and will not be lost. Barth is smeared with an anti-Semitic turn of phrase; Christ is persuaded that salvation is of the Jews. The sort of Bible that Barth saw as requiring a great act of divine humiliation to use, Christ saw as the Scripture which cannot be broken.

The great need of the day is not the humility of God to use a fallible Bible, but the humility of man to bow before the infallible and inspired Word of God. The choice before us is to accept either Christ's view of the Bible or man's.

3. To err is human

It has been argued that an infallible Bible is an impossibility because the doctrine of the Fall means that man always mars everything he touches. This is expressed in the proverb, 'To err is human.' A Bible written by men would have to reflect their human frailty and susceptibility to error.

Before the days of modern recording methods, some of us still remember winding up the gramophone and applying the horn containing the needle to our records! The result was often less than satisfactory. Even the best singers and orchestras sounded 'crackly'. The sounds were not clear. The art of recording was not well enough developed. It is argued that in the same way the voice of God can sound muffled and in some senses be hidden, when mediated through human writers.

While it is true that in this fallen world to err is human, it is not true that to err is *invariably* human. Human beings do sometimes get things right. A group of adults can usually be tested in basic mathematics and spellings without mistakes. The ability to get things right is also part of our humanity, for the powers of reason with which we were created have not been totally removed.

If we add to the human ability to sometimes get things right the power of God to sustain a person in making correct statements, then the possibility of an infallible Scripture is present. There is a hidden atheism in the suggestion that God could not enable men to record his Word without error.

The fact is that Scripture insists that prophets spoke from God as they were carried along by the Holy Spirit and that their words were God's words (2 Peter 1:20-21). The Scriptures also insist that the Scriptures, that is the *writings* themselves, and not merely the writers, are God-breathed (2 Tim. 3:16). Why should it be incredible to anyone that God should gain an accurate recording for the Scriptures?

The root of so many of the problems that modern man has with the Scriptures is found in his antipathy to all things supernatural. It is his substitute god, humanism, that blinds his eyes to the ability of the true God to do according to his will on earth or in heaven, with no one being able to stop him (Dan. 4:35). Man is constantly saying of God, 'He can't.' The proper response is: 'Why not?'

4. The phenomenon of error

Of late apologists for Islam have spent much time combing the Bible, and books about the Bible, to find errors. They have accumulated a list of problems with which they have armed their devotees to use in debates with Christians. Finding errors in the Bible has been a 'hobby' with various types of antagonists to the Bible throughout the centuries, but especially in the last 300 years.

One of the main ways that confidence in the authority of the Bible was undermined in the nineteenth century was to write about, or lecture on, the errors in the Scriptures — or should we not more accurately say, the supposed errors? There is, after all, a difference between a problem that is not yet solved and an error. An unsolved problem has a solution. An error cannot possibly be reconciled with fact under any circumstances.

Those who so confidently compose lists of 'errors' in today's world need to remember the track record of their forebears. Did not Julius Wellhausen, the most important of the German Higher Critics of the last century, confidently assert that Moses could not have written the Pentateuch because writing was not known in the days of Moses? Has not archaeology subsequently demonstrated that writing existed over 1,000 years before him? What scorn was poured upon the Bible for its mention of those totally unknown people the Hittites, until their empire was discovered! With what relish the historicity of Belshazzar was confidently denied, until the discovery of his name on cuneiform tablets! As the meaning of Scripture becomes clearer, the problems of Scripture become fewer.

Words written in another context are worth pondering when we are faced with a difficulty in the biblical text: 'The difficulty proceeds from our ignorance rather than our knowledge. The Divine wisdom is equal to the solution of the problem, and were we in possession of the requisite knowledge the discrepancy would melt away like the mist, and complete harmony would be disclosed between the seeming contradictions.'[3]

There are fundamentally two approaches to the difficulties which undoubtedly exist in Scripture:

1. I may begin with the problems, call them errors and decide that the phenomenon of error rules out the possibility of an inspired, infallible and inerrant Scripture. This begins with my ability to solve problems as the basis for belief. It is fundamentally humanistic.

2. I may begin with submission to the view of Scripture accepted by Christ and his apostles and conclude that therefore the Scriptures are inspired, infallible and inerrant. I will seek solutions to the problems that exist and do so trusting that there must be solutions. This view does not require me to accept unsatisfactory solutions, but to wait, if necessary, for more light to clarify the correct answer.[4]

The first of these approaches would be viewed by some people as more scientific, but it is not. If the Scriptures are the work of God, and Christ is behind the teaching of both the Old and New Testaments, it can hardly be a scientific procedure to ignore the Author's view in considering his Word!

It is also sometimes suggested that only a 'lunatic fringe' of obscurantists would now deny that there are errors in the Bible and that to hold to inerrancy is impossible for anyone who has 'half a brain'! The fact is that this is an untruth and a slander. However, those who associate themselves with the position taken by Christ, his apostles and the vast majority of Christian leaders throughout the Christian era must be willing, if necessary, to suffer abuse or sneering, patronizing comment from their opponents. To sell the truth for the sake of accept-ance by the scholastic establishment is to sell our birthright for a bowl of soup.

5. Limited inerrancy

An increasingly popular solution to the presence of problems within the Scriptures is to propose a doctrine of limited inerrancy. This argues that a distinction may be made between the Bible as a revelation of theological truth and as a record of facts. Its promoters contend that the Bible has no errors in its theology, although it can err in regard to its history, geography, chronology, etc.

The advantage of this view, as seen by its advocates, is that it enables the gospel and all the theological issues raised by Scripture to be maintained, but allows for errors in non-theo-logical material. This, it is argued, enables the Christian to argue over the important ground, but to give way on matters which are secondary.

Among the objections to this view there are several which make it untenable. It is our Christology, who Christ is, that makes limited inerrancy unacceptable. It is evident that our Lord made no such distinction in his treatment of the Old Tes-tament. Neither did his apostles. For them, Adam and Eve, and the events with which they were associated, were true (Matt. 19:1-6; Rom. 5:12-21). Jonah existed, and was swallowed by a fish (Luke 11:29-32). Sodom was destroyed and Lot's wife was turned to a pillar of salt (Luke 17:32). These were not simply theological ideas but historical events. In New Testament days this tendency to sever theology from history was a mark of heretics. Over against them the New Testament writers emphasized the historical reality of the things they believed (Luke 1:1-4; 2 Peter 1:16-21; 1 John 1:1-4).

It must also be recognized that the division suggested by the proponents of limited inerrancy is impossible. If we consider Genesis 1-11, who is to determine where the theology begins and the history ends? They are indivisibly woven together.

Limited inerrancy also lays itself open to the charge that it is constructed to save its proponents from embarrassment at having to defend Scripture, rather than being a serious theological option. It is effectively saying that if someone can find an error in the Bible then that part will be relegated to the secondary realm, but if there is no problem we will call it a theological part of Scripture. It is very convenient that where the factuality of the Bible can be tested (in its history, geography, chronology, science, etc.) it is to be termed errant and where it cannot be tested (in its theology) it is to be called inerrant!

This theory just will not do. It fails in its desire to have the best of both worlds. If we may borrow another idiomatic phrase, the person who advocates limited inerrancy wants 'to have his cake and eat it'. He must either have the courage of his convictions and stand shoulder to shoulder with Christ, the apostles and historic Christianity, or cross over to the other side and work hand in hand with the opponents of biblical authority.

Conclusion

All attitudes towards the Scriptures that are at variance with
that of Christ and his apostles cannot justly claim the name
'Christian'. In this matter, as in every other, the child of God
should be content to be conformed to the image of his Master.

The original text of Scripture

The church has never held the verbal infallibility of our translations, nor the perfect accuracy of the copies of the original Hebrew and Greek Scriptures now possessed by us. These copies confessedly contain many 'discrepancies' resulting from frequent transcription. It is, nevertheless, the unanimous testimony of Christian scholars that, while these variations embarrass the interpretation of many details, they neither involve the loss nor abate the evidence of a single essential fact or doctrine of Christianity. And it is moreover reassuring to know that believing criticism is constantly advancing to the possession of a more perfect text of the original Scriptures than she has enjoyed since the apostolic age.

A. A. Hodge

The true objective of the textual critic should be the restoration of the Hebrew to the point where it is as near as possible to what the original author is deemed to have written.

R. K. Harrison

Only about a thousandth part of the New Testament presents 'substantial variation' — i.e. variation which really alters the sense of the passage. It is on this thousandth part that the labours of New Testament textual criticism [have] been largely expended with excellent results. God, in his kind providence, has guarded his Word in such a manner that we can say, without fear of successful contradiction, that today we have an Old as well as a New Testament which is *substantially* as it was when it came forth from the pen of the inspired writers.

W. Hendriksen

6.
The original text of Scripture

The original Scriptures, or autographs, as they came from the hands of their writers, are no longer in our possession. We merely have copies, many copies which may be studied. This is true for both the Hebrew Old Testament and the Greek New Testament.

The absence of the originals ought not to surprise us, for if they still existed they, rather than their Author, would be worshipped and their fabric, rather than their content, would be honoured. The human tendency towards superstition is notorious!

The problem with any hand-copied document is that error occurs. Most of the variants in the manuscripts are of one of the following seven types:

1. The scribes failed to repeat a letter or word (haplography).

2. The scribes repeated what should have occurred only once (dittography).

3. The scribes included in the manuscript something occurring in a similar passage elsewhere, or in another manuscript, thus adding to the text.

4. The scribes omitted a passage between identical words.

5. The scribes omitted a line.
6. The scribes confused similar-looking letters.
7. The scribes inserted marginal notes into the text.

Discovering the correct text will involve some method of eliminating these errors. This activity is called 'textual criticism' and is an activity in which every Bible translator has to engage in order to have a text of the Bible from which to translate!

The Old Testament text

The Old Testament Hebrew text is represented in Hebrew manuscripts dating from the third century B.C. to the twelfth century A.D. There are also ancient versions in Aramaic, Greek, Latin and Syriac.

1. The Massoretic Text

Up to the twentieth century we only knew of one main tradition of Hebrew texts, named after the Massoretes, who were Jews responsible for the preservation of the Old Testament between A.D. 500 and 1000. This text came to be known as the Massoretic Text.

The Massoretes were very careful with the text and developed all sorts of procedures for detecting and eliminating variants. They counted the number of letters in each book, checked its middle letter and counted the words and the middle word of each book. Peculiarities in spelling were noted, as were peculiar words and phrases. In this way they guarded against scribal errors in the text.

2. The Dead Sea Scrolls

The discovery of the Dead Sea Scrolls in 1947 unearthed manuscripts a thousand years older than those preserved by the Massoretes. There was no shortage of scholars and pseudo-scholars who assured the world that the new discoveries would discredit the integrity of the Massoretic Text.

However, although there are some variations, many scholars have concluded that the Dead Sea Scrolls maintain the essential integrity of the Massoretic Text and, in fact, are an essential independent witness to its reliability and to the reliable copying which must have taken place in the thousand years for which we have no extant manuscripts.

3. The Samaritan Pentateuch

The Samaritan Pentateuch is an ancient edition of the first five books of Moses written in Hebrew. Its disagreement in various places with the Massoretic Text has endeared it to those who oppose the integrity of the traditional text. However, great care needs to be taken in using the Samaritan Pentateuch to correct the Massoretic Text because it is clear that the Samaritan scribes altered the text of the Pentateuch to suit their own historical and theological interests, and it contains other mistakes which are clearly the result of a misunderstanding of grammar and syntax.

Also, there is no evidence that the Samaritans ever had a body of trained scribes as the Jews did. Nor did they collate their manuscripts properly or reveal any serious textual knowledge. Their additions and carelessness with the text make reliance on their text a dangerous exercise.

4. The Septuagint

When we turn from Hebrew there are a number of versions of the Old Testament in Greek, Latin and Syriac and targums, or paraphrases, in Aramaic. These usually date from the Christian era, but one, the Septuagint (or *LXX*), predates the Christian era, having been commenced in the first half of the third century B.C. It was an attempt over a period of time to translate the Hebrew Bible into Greek for Greek-speaking Jews.

The Septuagint translation often suggests a different Hebrew text as its basis from the Massoretic text. Sometimes this is similar to what is found in the Samaritan Pentateuch, but often it is different. The problem, however, in assessing the underlying Hebrew text is the unevenness, even eccentricity, of the translation.

Sometimes the translation is little more than Hebraistic Greek. At other times it is free paraphrase. The Septuagint translators changed the text for reasons of theology, gave interpretations rather than translations, reinstated the characters of some of those criticized in the Hebrew text and made various conjectures. Its use to correct the Massoretic Text is, therefore, something which needs to be approached with great caution.

In finding a text from which to translate the Old Testament, it is wisest to stay with the Massoretic Text and to use the other materials as comparative aids, but not as the basis for changes.

The New Testament text[1]

The New Testament text, in whole or in part, is found in over 5,000 Greek manuscripts — translations of all sorts from the early centuries, books of Bible readings for early church use and numerous quotations from the early Church Fathers. These sources of evidence for the New Testament text range from the second to the sixteenth century in their dating.

The problem with the New Testament manuscripts is that no two are exactly the same. Every manuscript has oddities of its own. Altogether, there are hundreds of thousands of variants. Before we become too alarmed, however, it needs to be recognized that most of these variants are easily recognizable as an obvious form of scribal error and can be seen to be mistakes rather than a part of the real text of the New Testament.

Nevertheless, there is a dispute over a minority of the text: some would say as little as 3%; others would talk in terms of 7-8%. The question which arises is how we are to determine the correct text in the areas where there are disagreements. There are five main approaches.

1. Follow the Received Text

The 'Received Text', or *Textus Receptus*, is a title given to the text of the Greek New Testament published by the Elzevir brothers in 1633. They coined the term to support their claim that their Greek text was the text that was generally accepted by the scholars of the day. In England a similar title was applied to the text published by Stephens in 1550. The only meaning that the Elzevir brothers gave to the phrase was that all the scholars of the day accepted this text. It was 'received' by them — not from God, or antiquity, or anything else. The retention of this title and the aura that accompanies it makes it one of the most successful pieces of publisher's advertising of all time.

The 'Received Text' is basically the text compiled by Erasmus in 1516. He created it by a comparison of six manuscripts and checked and amended it by reference to the Latin

Vulgate, from which he constructed a small part of the text for which he lacked any Greek manuscript.

If we are to follow the Received Text slavishly, then we argue that Erasmus' decisions were correct even when the majority of the manuscripts and the earliest manuscripts disagree with him. We are insisting on following the text he made up from the Latin even where there is no Greek evidence at all to support him. To follow the Received Text is to ignore all other evidence and to invest in the infallibility of Erasmus.

2. Follow Westcott and Hort

In the nineteenth century the textual critics Westcott and Hort set out to establish a text on other principles than those used by Erasmus, and made their starting-point a hatred of the Received Text.

They argued that where manuscripts had the same variants they had to be related and, therefore, they felt able to divide the manuscripts into families. Each family was a representative text type, however large or small it might be.

Westcott and Hort had a special liking for what they termed the 'Neutral Text', a very small set of witnesses largely dependent on two early manuscripts known as Sinaiticus and Vaticanus.

If we follow Westcott and Hort slavishly then we are arguing that their decisions were correct even when the majority of the manuscripts are against them. The infallibility of Erasmus' six manuscripts is replaced by the tyranny of Westcott and Hort's two. Virtually all other evidence is rendered irrelevant.

3. Follow subjective opinions

In the twentieth century two scholars, G. D. Kilpatrick and J. K. Elliot, have developed a third approach to textual variants.

They determine the correct reading by answering just two questions. They ask, firstly, 'Which variant best suits the context?' and, secondly, 'Which variant best explains all the other variants?' No other evidence is taken into consideration at all.

The highly subjective nature of this method is immediately apparent. The New Testament text is to be determined by my opinion as to which variant I think would fit the rest of the text and explain the alternatives. The infallibility of Erasmus is replaced, not with the two infallible manuscripts of Westcott and Hort, but with the opinions of anyone who wants to make a case for a particular variant. This is the ultimate in subjectivity.

4. Follow the majority reading

An increasingly popular and simple method of cutting through the whole problem of weighing the evidence in any way for a particular reading is to count the number of manuscripts in favour of a variant. It could not be simpler!

However, there is some unease about establishing something on the basis of the opinion of the majority. Is the majority always right? If we did this with the text of the Latin Vulgate we would undoubtedly end up with an inferior text. Is it safe to follow a majority reading even though there may be no evidence for its existence before the fourth century? Are we simply to count and ignore evidence? Although this approach has its attractions, is it not just too easy?

5. Follow the variants that satisfy most principles

During the twentieth century an approach to the New Testament text has been developed which is termed 'eclecticism'. This refers to the selection of a variant from among others on the basis of reasonable principles. These principles divide into two groups: external considerations and internal considerations.

The external considerations are three:

1. Has this variant ancient support?
2. Has this reading geographical support — i.e. is it found in various different parts of the world?
3. How does the evidence in support of it compare with the evidence in support of other variants?

The internal considerations are five:

1. Which variant would be the most difficult for the scribe to accept and, therefore, most likely to be replaced by him?
2. When there is a longer and a shorter reading, is there any evidence of an accidental omission due to a slip of the eye? Is the omitted material something that a scribe would have omitted because it seems superfluous, or harsh, or contrary to orthodox belief or practice? If not, the shorter reading is to be preferred.
3. When there is a variant in a passage which involves a quotation from the Old Testament, or which has a parallel New Testament passage, then the scribe is more likely to harmonize than to disharmonize, so the less harmonized variant is probably wrong.
4. Variants creating a more rugged text are more likely to be authentic than smooth readings which involve no difficulties.
5. Variants which best fit the immediate and general contexts are to be accepted over against other variants.

These principles are not infallible. The external principles are stronger than the internal. There is a considerable element of subjectivity in the internal principles. The assertion that scribes would have done this or that is ultimately only an assumption. Those who have studied scribal habits are not entirely agreed as to what the evidence suggests about their habits. To speak of 'the assured results' of textual criticism seems an over-confident assertion.

Bible versions today and the texts

Most modern translators have opted for a New Testament text based on eclectic principles. Some maintain the Received Text. There are no major translations at the moment based on the other three approaches.

Perhaps the best thing that readers of Bible versions can do is to recognize the complexity of the problems of textual decisions and remember that the motivation of most Bible translators is not a desire to be perverse, or to destroy much-loved texts, but to restore the true New Testament text. The fact is that there is no infallible way of proving which approach is correct. Disagreements over the correct text are, therefore, inevitable. Abuse of those who differ seems hardly appropriate. Understanding and discussion of the choices seems more suited to those who share a common view of Scripture and a common salvation in Christ.

The translation of Scripture

Although their utility is great for the instruction of believers, yet no version either can or ought to be put on an equality with the original, much less preferred to it.

Francis Turretin

No translation is ever final. Because translators are human beings, there will always be room for improvements of translations. No translator can transcend his own time; he can only work in light of the knowledge of his day, with materials available to him, and put his translation in words spoken by his generation.

Neil R. Lightfoot

The Bible in translation is the Word of God to the extent that the translated text conforms to what was originally written in the autographs... Any translation is liable to suffer from two opposite defects which need to be kept firmly in mind:

(a) In the process of translation ideas and approaches which are not contained in the original may be superadded to it so as to burden the original message with certain elements which are not found in the autographs;

(b) in the process of translation certain ideas, overtones or connotations which are suggested by the original text may be lost sight of so that the translated message impoverishes in some respect the autographic text.

One who uses the Scripture through translation will therefore be careful to guard against this double danger.

Roger Nicole

7.
The translation of Scripture

The revelation which God has given of himself and which is recorded in the Scriptures is of limited use to the people of the world if it is locked away in the original languages — Hebrew, Aramaic and Greek. Historically, some branches of Christendom and some scholars have been very pleased to have the Scriptures kept away from the masses because this leaves the interpretation of the Scriptures in the hands of self-declared 'experts' only.

The Scriptures themselves, however, declare in various ways that they ought to be available to the people of the earth and in their languages. The fact that God has given a revelation of himself in Scripture means that he wants to make himself known to his creatures. To hide the Scriptures from the people is, therefore, to oppose God!

Those who tested the apostle Paul's preaching at Berea by comparing it with the Scriptures are commended (Acts 17:11). Their good example can only be followed if the Scriptures can be read by the hearers of preaching.

John's Gospel was written as an evangelistic tool to bring his readers to faith in Christ Jesus (John 20:31). His aim would be frustrated if the knowledge of Christ which he imparts in his Gospel could not be read.

The blessings of the book of Revelation are promised to those who read and hear its words (Rev. 1:3). If the Scriptures are locked away in foreign languages the blessing must be missed.

It is irrefutably clear that the original Scriptures were never written to experts but to individuals and churches. They were not written in highly intellectual language, but in the language of the people. Therefore, the Scriptures written for the people must be made available to the people in their language.

Some guiding principles

Our doctrine of Scripture ought to determine our translation procedures. Humanists do not make good Bible translators because they have no insight into the truth of the book they are translating. The spiritually dead are not useful translators of the Word of life.

Bible-believing people, however, do not automatically make good translators. The principles that guide them in translation are very important. Good men may work with bad principles. The following paragraphs list some of the important guiding principles for translators.

1. Remember the implications of the fact that the Bible is God's Word

Translators of any human writing should take the utmost care in translating the original work. How much more should a Bible translator take care when dealing with God-breathed Scriptures!

In the modern world many Bible translators have shifted the emphasis from God, the giver of Scripture, to man, the receiver. The understanding of the Bible reader has become all-important. Communication has become a 'god' and the message communicated has become secondary. A proper regard for the Bible as God's Word ought to restrain this tendency and cause the translator to regard it as his highest duty to represent faithfully what God has said, even if that leaves some things a little ambiguous and in need of clarification by preachers and commentators.

2. Remember the implications of verbal inspiration

A Bible that is verbally inspired — given in the words God wants to convey his message — is a different type of literature from a book which is correct in its general argument but not in its detail.

While it is true that no language can be translated into another language word for word and make sense, because each language has its own form and grammar, translators have to make sure that they convey the *exact* sense of the original in their language form, and not merely the *general* sense, and that they convey *no more than* the original language.

Bible translators have a very difficult tightrope to walk. The modern tendency is to slip over far too often from being translators to being interpreters. What is ambiguous in the original language should be ambiguous in the receptor language. What is hard to understand in the original should be hard to understand in the translation (see 2 Peter 3:16).

3. Remember the type of language God used

The Bible could have been written in a high style of Hebrew, Greek and Aramaic. The literati of the first century wrote their books in a type of Attic Greek. The original Bible was not written in a high literary style beyond the reach of ordinary people. Nor was the Bible written in the language of today's newspaper, a type of urban slang. It was language, not 'slanguage'!

The Bible was written in the language of the ordinary man. Very few of its words are of its own creation. The language of the Bible is the language of the people. Of course, all of us use a wide variety of words. The language of the people has a very extensive vocabulary. It is not all words of one syllable; nor is it devoid of technical terms and specialized uses. Therefore, the Bible has to be written in a good quality but common style. The desire to make a literary masterpiece out of a translation or to make it on a level with the 'gutter press' are desires contrary to the intentions of God the giver.

To put these general principles into practice is no easy thing. A good Bible translator wants to convey God's Word in his own language accurately, but what is accuracy?

The definition of accuracy

Bible translators have genuine differences of opinion over the nature of accuracy in five areas.

1. Accuracy and language form

The whole nature of a Bible translation is determined by the answer to one question: 'Is the translation into English (or another local language) to be ruled by the grammar and construction of the original language, in so far as that is possible, or is the structure of the original language to be reconstructed in the form of the receptor language?'

For example, in the original languages of the Bible there are long sentences which are often endlessly joined together by the use of words meaning 'and'. There are also double negatives for emphasis. In modern English, however, sentences tend to be shorter. Sentences beginning with 'and' are not approved. Double negatives give a positive sense. Is the translator to produce a Hellenized form of English, or Anglicized Greek? The answer to this question makes a profound difference to the style of the translation. Which is more accurate?

2. Formal equivalence, dynamic equivalence and paraphrase

'Formal equivalence' means that the translator seeks, wherever it is possible, to give an exact equivalent in the receptor language to each word in the original language.

'Dynamic equivalence' means that the translator seeks to express what is said in the original language in the way that it would have been said if originally written in the receptor language.

'Paraphrase' means that the original words are explained, simplified and developed so as to convey the maximum understanding of the intention of the original writer.

It has to be accepted as an incontrovertible fact that formal equivalence cannot always occur. No two languages are exactly parallel, word for word. Therefore, all translations contain some element of dynamic equivalence. However, there is a large area of variation among translators as to the degree to which this element is used. It has to be recognized that the more a dynamic equivalent is sought, or the more a passage is paraphrased, the greater is the degree of subjective interpretation in the translation.

For a large part of the Bible, formal equivalence is possible. Where it can be used, it should be. It is a fact, however, that dynamic equivalence is also necessary sometimes. In the end, any translation can only be partially accurate.

3. The use of technical language

A few modern translations abandon technical language and seek to give simplified definitions to words such as propitiation, redemption, justification, etc. The argument is that modern men do not understand these terms, so they have to be explained.

The fact is that such words were just as technical and theological to the Hebrews and Greeks to whom they were first written as they are to us. As in the original languages, there was a certain irreducible amount of words which are so packed with meaning and significance that it is inevitable that any attempted simplification will reduce their meaning and create a false understanding. Every department of human learning has a certain number of technical terms in its textbooks and Christianity is no different in that respect.

Perhaps the best solution to the translator's dilemma is to retain technical terms in the text but to give definitions in the margin where available, or to leave that as part of the work of the preacher. It is worse to have an inadequate definition in the text, which gives it an air of authority, than to leave in place a complex word which needs further study and definition by the use of aids outside of the Bible itself.

4. Cross-cultural terms

Biblical people were used to cubits, the denarius, the ephah etc. Their weights and measures are not ours. Some Bible translators leave these alien names in the text and give notes, or leave the reader to find out the meaning in some other way. Others try to assist the reader by giving modern equivalents. The problem with this latter approach is that inflation changes money values and the government has, in Britain at least, spent much of the last few decades changing weights and measures. In the average congregation some are confused if the Bible reading mentions feet and inches, pounds and pence, while the rest still struggle with metres and litres, pounds and 'p'! There is no easy answer to this problem nor any infallible definition of accuracy in this matter.

5. The second person singular

One issue which affects the whole way in which a version is translated is the understanding of the significance of the second person singular. Is it to be translated 'thee' and thou', with the associated word forms, or as 'you'?

Considered as a translation issue *alone*, the answer is not complicated. In modern English 'thee' and 'thou' are no longer in use and, being obsolete, have no place in a modern English translation, unless we adopt the view that the original languages must control the receptor language, even to the degree of imposing archaic forms upon it.

Supplementary arguments based on tradition or archaic forms as an aid to reverence, while not totally irrelevant to a wider issue, are not really to the point when translational factors alone are being considered. They are not scriptural arguments, but subjective or historical. The sensitivity of this issue in the eyes of some makes it the controlling factor in some arguments over translations, but it ought rather to be a factor, not the determining issue.

These five major problems are at the heart of the translator's concerns. Whatever decisions he makes on these matters will affect the sort of translation he produces, and our opinion of them will affect the choice of translation which we make.

Translation choices[1]

Not everyone is guided by principles in choosing a translation. Prejudices can also play a large part. Some people have a character which hates anything that is new and must abuse it. Others are so unstable that they always welcome everything new and detest everything old and must attack it. We must distinguish in our assessment of translations between the comments of those ruled by prejudice and those governed by principles.

Some are guided in their choice of translation purely by tradition. They love the Bible they have used for years, whatever version it may be, and see no reason to change. Such people should allow others freedom to make choices also and to find a favourite version.

Those, however, who want to be guided by principles must decide on which side of the argument over the nature of accuracy they align themselves. Then they need to weigh how each version applies those principles and which most corresponds to them. A choice of a translation because of well-considered principles will be a rewarding activity. It is to be hoped that each person will be allowed to make his or her choice without being subjected to abuse from those who differ.

The sufficiency of Scripture

My assurances are not the marvels of Merlin, nor yet the dark sentences of profane prophecies; but the plain truth of God's Word, the invincible justice of the everlasting God, and the ordinary course of his punishments and plagues from the beginning are my assurances and grounds.

John Knox

What wise man is there in the world that will or dare lay and venture his soul upon a dream and the interpretation of it? But you may and must lay and venture your souls and salvation upon the Scripture.

William Bridge

Scripture records the direct revelations which God gave to men in days past so far as these revelations were intended for permanent and universal use. But it is much more than a record of past revelations. It is itself the final revelation of God, completing the whole discourse of his unfathomable love to lost sinners, the whole proclamation of the purpose of grace, and the whole exhibition of his gracious provisions for their salvation.

Benjamin Warfield

8.
The sufficiency of Scripture

Before they met Jesus, the apostles, as Jews, had the Holy Scriptures of the Old Testament. During his earthly ministry Christ taught them all that they could absorb at that time. At his ascension he sent them his Holy Spirit to remind them of all that he had taught them and to lead them into 'all truth'.

'All truth' was not everything that they wanted to know, but everything that Christ wanted them to know, and that they needed to know, to please God. 'All truth' is the truth in all its parts, the whole body of redemptive truth.

While the apostles lived they passed on this truth by preaching and writing. It was natural, however, that people would begin to be fearful about what would happen to the truth after their demise. Timid people like Timothy were particularly concerned. For this reason, Paul wrote his last and most reassuring letter to him, directing him away from timidity and showing him where to look for all truth once the apostles had gone (1 Tim. 4:12; 2 Tim. 1:7-8; 2:1).

The Scriptures: the depository of all truth (2 Tim. 3:14-17)

From infancy Timothy had been taught the 'sacred writings' (v. 15). Paul did not use the usual term for Scripture here, but a term in common use among the Jews to describe the Old Testament, and one which is found on a number of occasions in the writings of Josephus. Timothy was encouraged to continue in the sacred writings, the Scriptures, which are a Christ-revealing book (Luke 24:27,44-45).

From the Old Testament Scriptures, Paul turned Timothy's attention to 'all Scripture' (v. 16), using the more familiar term. Many have wanted to make the 'sacred writings' and 'all Scripture' co-extensive. Sometimes this is with the aim of asserting that it was impossible that in the apostles' lifetimes their writings could have been regarded as Scripture. However, not only is it clear that Paul refers to Luke's Gospel and Peter to Paul's letters as Scripture (1 Tim. 5:18; 2 Peter 3:16), but there is no necessary improbability in their so doing, for it is clear that the apostles considered their writings to have special authority and expected their readers to recognize the fact. For this reason, there is no surprise that in the days after the apostles, the churches had no difficulty in treating the apostolic writings as of equal authority to the Old Testament because the apostles and their readers did this themselves.

Far from wanting to identify the 'sacred writings' and 'all Scripture', Paul uses the expression 'sacred writings' in verse 15, but 'all Scripture' in verse 16, in order to draw a distinction between the Old Testament and whatever has a right to be called divinely inspired Scripture. The latter includes more than the former.

Timothy must pay attention, not merely to the Old Testament, with which he had been familiar since childhood, but to all Scripture. For all Scripture, whether the Old Testament, or the Gospels, or the epistles, was God-breathed and profitable to teach, rebuke, correct and instruct in righteousness, in all that is pleasing to God (v. 16).

How adequate is all Scripture to teach and guide in the things that please God? Timothy is told that all Scripture is profitable so that the man of God might be complete (Greek, *artios,* v. 17). This word, used only here in the New Testament, has the meaning elsewhere of 'suitable', 'correct' or 'normal'. The idea in this passage is that the man of God is made able to meet all the demands of the situation. The Scriptures 'tool up' a man for the work of pleasing God.

This word is followed by a related verb in an intensive form. The man of God is equipped, or fitted out, for his work (Greek, *exartizo,* v. 17). The Scriptures 'tool up' and 'fit out' a man for the work of pleasing God. They provide the information he needs to believe and obey in order to serve God.

Are the Scriptures partially or totally adequate for this task? Paul was in no doubt and wrote dogmatically and unequivocally. The Scriptures 'tool up' and 'fit out' the man of God for '*every* good work' (v. 17).

To be good a work must proceed from faith, be commanded by God and be done for his glory. The Scriptures teach a man what God requires of him. There is no doctrine which needs to be believed, or duty which needs to be fulfilled, about which Scripture does not give us adequate information to enable us to believe and obey God.

In his teaching to Timothy, Paul was establishing the same principle as that which came into effect when the succession of Old Testament prophets ceased and the inter-testamental period began. At the end of the Old Testament period the Word of God no longer came through the voice of man but in the written Word. The demise of the apostles brought about that situation again. Just as the truth once revealed through Moses, the prophets and their wise men of old was deposited in the Old Testament Scriptures, so the truth revealed through Christ, the apostles and prophets of the New Testament age was deposited in the New Testament.

Once the apostolic voice was silenced, 'all truth' was not lost but was found in 'all Scripture'. Failure to appreciate this was a disastrous mistake for the churches in the centuries that followed the apostles. Although they made appeal to a two-fold witness of the Old Testament and the testimony of the apostles, they failed to limit this witness to the written testimony of the apostles and accepted a tradition passed on and preserved by the church. Soon greater importance began to be attached to this tradition than to the apostolic Scriptures, and the churches slid into captivity to the authority of church tradition and ultimately to that tradition as interpreted in Rome by the pope.

It was the glory of the Protestant Reformation to dethrone the pope, the Roman church and tradition, and to reassert the authority of God's Word. 'The Reformers' whole understanding of Christianity depended on the principle of *sola Scriptura*: that is, the view that the Scripture, as the *only* Word of God in this world, is the *only* guide for conscience and the church, the *only* source of true knowledge of God and grace, and the *only* qualified judge of the church's testimony and teaching, past and present.'[1]

If the Scriptures are the only teacher of what we need to believe and obey to please God, what are the implications of this doctrine and how may it be put into practice?

The implications of sufficiency for continuing prophecy

As the Scriptures teach us all we need to know to please God, we have no need of continuing prophecy. The inter-testamental Jews did not need prophecy when they had the Old Testament Scriptures. We do not need prophecy now we have the New Testament Scriptures.

This conclusion has always been resisted by some, and never more so than in the modern world. Some have wanted to encourage continuing prophecy. In support of this they argue that although the inter-testamental Jews did not have prophecy in its full Old Testament sense, they did affirm the existence of revelatory phenomena of a supernatural sort in the inter-testamental period.

These 'revelatory phenomena' are not without their difficulties. There is great hesitancy and uncertainty even among those who produce this evidence. They are not sure whether these revelatory phenomena should be called 'prophecy', or 'quasi-prophetic activity', or 'a sort of prophetic sense'. They concur in recognizing that these phenomena were inferior to the prophecy found in the Old Testament and have to concede that there is no certainty that they actually occurred. This hesitancy and uncertainty should be weighed.

Further, we must ask whether it logically follows that, because some inter-testamental Jews believed that a certain amount of quasi-prophetic activity of inferior quality occurred among them in spite of the cessation of Old Testament prophecy and the close of the canon of Old Testament Scripture, we should accept the continuance of New Testament prophecy? Especially we should note that, whatever some Jews did or did not believe, our Lord saw 'the Prophets and the Law' as prophesying 'until John' (Matt. 11:13), and nothing else. For him the written Word prophesied, not the quasi-prophetic revelatory phenomena!

However, the advocates of continuing prophecy insist that it must continue because they argue there is no indication in the New Testament that it would cease. Is there not?

Does not Paul tell us that the church is built upon the foundation of the apostles and prophets? (Eph. 2:20). It will not do to interpret these prophets as Old Testament prophets because in the epistle to the Ephesians Paul draws a contrast between the truth revealed in past ages and that which is *'now'* (in the first century) revealed to his apostles and prophets (Eph. 3:4-7). These prophets are New Testament prophets and, with the apostles, are the foundation of the church, not part of its continuing ministry.

Various attempts are made to undermine the significance of this passage. It is argued that it is not the apostles and prophets as persons that are in view but their teaching. Their doctrine is the foundation on which the church is built. However, a study of the context of Ephesians 2:20 makes it clear that the 'building' being described consists of people only: the Ephesians (who were predominantly Gentiles), the Jewish believers, Christ, the apostles and the prophets. A sudden change from people to doctrine would be a violent destruction of the whole picture.

Others argue that the Greek of Ephesians 2:20 ought to be translated 'the apostles who are prophets', thus making the apostles alone foundational and enabling a continuing ministry of prophets. Now such a translation, while possible, is not necessary and is ruled out by the wider context of Ephesians. In his list of Christ's gifts to the church, Paul clearly distinguishes prophets from apostles (Eph. 4:11). Are we to argue that what is distinguished in chapter 4 is confused and mingled in chapters 2 and 3? (Eph. 2:20; 3:5). Surely not!

The New Testament prophets with the New Testament apostles are the foundation on which the church is built, not part of a superstructure that is still being erected. Apostolic-prophetic ministries of the spoken word have given way to apostolic-prophetic teaching in written Scripture.

The implications of sufficiency for dreams

The Scriptures undoubtedly teach that God used dreams to reveal his will to his people, and sometimes even to the heathen in the days of the Old Testament and in the apostolic age (Num. 12:6; Acts 2:17). The arrival of 'all Scripture', however, makes revelatory dreams unnecessary.

Inevitably strong objection is made to such a statement by those who profess to have God-given dreams, and their claims need analysis and response.

What causes dreams? Let me suggest and illustrate five causes.

1. God's revelatory activity

Revelatory dreams were such an important part of prophetic experience that even the false prophets knew they had to claim to have had a dream if their claim to be prophets was to be considered credible (Num. 12:6; Jer. 23:25-28). However, having 'all truth', we no longer need such continuing revelation by dream.

2. Satan's hostile attacks

In his suffering Job complained about the fact that he had experienced terrible torment through dreams (Job 7:14). Although Job blamed God for these dreams, we remember that he did not have the insight which we have into Job 1-2 to know that, in fact, he had been handed over to the attacks of Satan. A natural phenomenon such as a dream can be used by Satan to cause us to wake distressed and oppressed. We need to ask God to protect us in our sleeping as well as our waking thoughts.

3. Natural causes

The story is told of a lady who asked a preacher to interpret a dream which she described in some detail and with some degree of spiritual pride. He gave her the following withering explanation: 'Too much cucumber in your sandwich before going to bed!'

Some dreams, even those which seem so very special, are able to be explained on the basis of purely natural causes. A full stomach or unwise eating can cause troublesome dreams. Of course, it is more 'spiritual' to attribute our dreams to God than to cucumber, but not necessarily more accurate!

4. Preceding thoughts and anxieties

How often my mother would tell me as a child that she had gone to bed thinking about all the washing that needed to be done the next day and had dreamt that she had done it. Waking up made clear the dreadful reality — it had only been a dream!

The worries, burdens, anxieties, joys and anticipations which fill the mind before sleep can often recur in the mind during sleep. Therefore, spiritual thoughts may create spiritual dreams without these being revelatory or in any special sense 'from God'.

5. God's activity in providence

God is very merciful to us and often has given special help to those whose faith is weak and faltering (Judg. 7:9-15; John 20:26-28). Sometimes when people are worried about something, God superintends the thoughts of their sleeping minds in such a way so as to give them peace rather than anxiety. Some who have been struggling with assurance of salvation have had their anguished hearts stilled by a dream. That God mercifully provides such dreams by ordering our thoughts to suit our needs cannot be denied, but we should neither call such an experience 'revelation', nor should we rely on it. It is as if the sides of a wound were being held together to stop bleeding — a temporary expedient, until better, more secure treatment can be found.

C. H. Spurgeon wisely counselled a lady who was assured of her salvation through a dream that although the dream may have been of use to her in doing her good she should not rely on it. A more solid ground for assurance should be sought in the teaching that the Scriptures give and the marks of the saved which they reveal. The tests of life given in 1 John are more reliable than a dream, which could have multiple causes, only one of which may be God. The certainties of Scripture should be trusted rather than the uncertainties of dreams.

The implications of sufficiency for impressions

Sometimes Christians get a very strong impression, feeling, or conviction that they ought to do something, or that something is happening, or is going to happen. These 'impressions' can prompt them to act in a certain way and, if expressed to others, can seem to be strongly 'of God'.

When C. H. Spurgeon felt that he ought to visit a particular person's house he did so in case this 'feeling' was the direction of God. Men like John Knox and Alexander Peden used to get strong impressions about present or future events and would sometimes express these to their associates. Their use and expression of their impressions had two effects. On the one hand, their devotees often suggested that they were 'prophets' and, on the other hand, their enemies accused them of presumptuously and arrogantly claiming entrance into the secret counsels of God. They denied both interpretations of their impressions.

In responding to the undoubted occurrence of such 'impressions', we need to notice certain important restraints.

Firstly, the famous men we have mentioned, who had these impressions, were themselves very hesitant to claim anything supernatural about them. They were hesitant to say that their impressions were always of God. They argued that to a large degree their insights and impressions, which others called prophecies, were based on their observance of God's justice and providence and their study of God's Word. History interpreted by Scripture led them to many of their conclusions and the guidance of the Spirit led them to some of their actions.

Secondly, these men gained a great many enthusiastic followers who loved nothing more than to exalt their heroes by remembering, exaggerating and manufacturing stories about their heroes and their powers. In the modern world, stories about Dr Lloyd-Jones, and what he said and did, are still a growth industry in some circles. Getting beyond the storytellers to the truth is sometimes difficult! Dr Lloyd-Jones only died in 1981.

Thirdly, there have been too many tragic examples of those who gave divine authority to their 'impressions' and lived to regret it (or sometimes died because of it). Even the great George Whitefield was self-deluded on one occasion. 'Following his child's birth Whitefield held a service at the Tabernacle in which he made known his impression that the child would grow up "to be a preacher of the everlasting Gospel" and in view of his assurance gave him the name "John".' But within a few days the child died. From then on Whitefield was more cautious about impressions.[2]

Such caution is well-founded. 'Impressions' that I ought to do something are notoriously subjective, both in being experienced and in their results. Of course, I may be 'moved by the Spirit' to do or say something (Luke 2:27). The sufficiency of Scripture does not cancel out the need for providential guidance. The interpretation of providential guidance is often difficult.

If I receive the 'impression' that I ought to do or say something, it would be dangerous to define the ignoring of such an impression as 'sin' or as 'quenching the Spirit'. To take no notice of it may be a mistake, but even that is not certain. Sin has to do with disobedience to God's law, which is objective, not with response to impressions, which are subjective.

When a man has a strong impression that something will happen, expresses it and is proved to be correct, it does not make him a prophet. A God-given insight which I express is not to be confused with God-inspired speech. Man's words prompted by knowledge granted by God are not the same as God's words spoken by man. In the discussion of the gift of continuing prophecy this distinction is constantly ignored.

In Paul's list of spiritual gifts in his first letter to the Corinthians the 'word of wisdom' and 'word of knowledge' are clearly distinguished from 'prophecy' (1 Cor. 12:8-10). The modern debate confuses these and makes them synonymous. These New Testament gifts are paralleled in the Old Testament by 'the secret of the Lord' which is 'with them that fear him' (Ps. 25:14).

Those who reject continuing prophecy altogether have no difficulty with this concept. Two respected commentators state that 'The man that feareth God shall know more of God's mind than others shall,'[3] and that 'They understand his word … they know the meaning of his providence.'[4]

Is such a special insight inconsistent with the sufficiency of Scripture? Thomas M'Crie, biographer of John Knox, wrote, 'The canon of our faith is contained in the Scripture of the Old and New Testament; we must not look to impressions or new revelations as the rule of our duty; but that God may, on particular occasions, forewarn people of some things that shall happen, to testify his approbation of them, to encourage them to confide in him in particular circumstances, or for other useful purposes, is not, I think, inconsistent with the principles of either natural or revealed religion.'[5]

What authority did these impressions, or intimations, have for the great men of old? 'Whatever intimations of this kind they enjoyed, they did not trust the authority of their mission upon them, nor appeal to them as constituting any part of the evidence of the doctrines which they preached to the world.'[6] It was the Scriptures alone which taught them what to believe and do to please God, but 'the secret of the Lord', or 'a word of knowledge', could be their encouragement.

The sufficiency of the Scriptures in practice

When we seek to put the sufficiency of Scripture into practice, what is involved? There are four things which we need to look for in Scripture in order to know what we are to believe and do.

1. A command

There are some things which God in his Word has commanded us to do. They are not obscure or unclear. We do not have to ask whether the commands of God are to be obeyed or not. Rather we show our love to him by obeying his commands joyfully (John 14:23; 1 John 5:3).

2. A prohibition

Some commands are positive; some are negative. There are things we are not to do. The modern obsession with being positive does not fit into a biblical context. The gospel teaches us to say 'No' to some things and 'Yes' to others (Titus 2:12; Eph. 4:29-30).

3. An example

The large amount of historical narrative which is found in the Scriptures, both Old and New, embodies in real-life situations the outworking of faith. All that is written is there to teach us, and one of the main methods of teaching is by example, whether for encouragement or warning (Rom. 15:4; 1 Cor. 10:6,11). Of course, only by interpreting the examples in accordance with the commands and prohibitions of Scripture can the decision be made whether the example is good or bad, unless there is something explicitly stated in the text.

4. A principle

Paul draws principles out of Scripture in order to direct behaviour. An Old Testament law about not muzzling oxen as they tread out the corn is used to demonstrate the principle that those who preach the gospel should live by the gospel (1 Cor. 9:8-14). Even where the Scripture does not give a command, prohibition or example, there is always a principle for each and every situation in an ever-changing world.

To use these commands, prohibitions, examples and principles properly three things are needed.

1. Prayer

The Scriptures are not automatically understood, either by the casual reader or by the intellectual student. Not only do they contain some things which are hard to understand (2 Peter 3:16), but Scripture can only be understood properly by those to whom the Spirit of God gives spiritual discernment (1 Cor. 2:14). Unless God opens the eyes of the reader the wonderful truths of Scripture will remain hidden. For this God-given illumination we must pray (Ps. 119:18).

2. Study

Even in apostolic days those who would understand and explain the Word had to study. Paul encouraged Timothy to give himself to the wholehearted study of the Scriptures so that his progress would be obvious and he need not be ashamed (1 Tim. 4:11-16; 2 Tim. 2:15). There is no short-cut to study. It takes time, thought, meditation and energy. Our 'instant' age will always have those who prefer an instant 'prophecy' to the study of the infallible Word of God.

3. Proper hermeneutics

Hermeneutics, the principles of interpretation, are exceedingly important. A command or doctrine which is misunderstood can do untold harm and damage. Whenever the apostle Paul realized that he had been misunderstood he was concerned to clarify the situation so as to leave his readers in no doubt about his true intention. When the Corinthians misapplied his teaching on church discipline to create a semi-monasticism he corrected their misinterpretation as quickly and clearly as possible (1 Cor. 5:9-13).

Proper hermeneutics are going to require a careful and honest handling of the Scriptures. This will involve questions about the type of literature being considered — is it prose or poetry, history or allegory? — questions about the context, parallel passages in the Scriptures, the type of language used, figures of speech, etc. All these principles aim at getting to the true meaning so that the correct application can be made. This involves hard work, but is necessary if God's will is to be discerned.

Why is the sufficiency of Scripture so important?

As in the Scriptures we are taught all that we need to know in order to believe and do all that pleases God, four important consequences follow.

1. Only from the Scriptures may we bind other people's consciences, or our own, as to what is to be believed

When we are challenged that we must believe such and such an idea if we would please God, we have every right to require proof from God's Word that it is a belief required by God. Where there is no biblical proof, there can be no requirement.

The attitude of C. H. Spurgeon ought to be ours: 'If God teaches it, it is enough. If it is not in the Word, away with it, away with it! But if it be in the Word, agreeable or disagreeable, systematic or disorderly, I believe it.'[7]

We will bind ourselves by what God requires us to believe in his Word, the Bible, but by no mere man-required belief. We need to distinguish between the commandments of men and the commandments of God (Matt. 15:9).

2. Only from the Scriptures may we bind other people's consciences, or our own, as to what is to be practised

When faced with Roman Catholic practices in the Church of England, which had no scriptural warrant, the early Puritan William Turner responded: 'Almighty God told his Son Christ all laws that [were] necessary for Christ's church, and Christ taught his apostles all that he heard from his Father, and all that the apostles learned from Christ necessary for Christ's church they and the evangelists have written in the New Testament which is the law of the gospel. But the evangelists and apostles have made no mention of the pope's ceremonies, laws and traditions; therefore they are not necessary for Christ's church, but the law of the gospel is necessary alone.'[8]

This is precisely correct. I can be required to obey no practice which God's Word does not require. Christians do not worship God or serve him according to man-made rules (Col. 2:20-23).

3. Only Scripture may define sin

That Christ's disciples should have kept the Sabbath in accordance with God's law is not in doubt. However, plucking ears of corn while walking through the fields on the Sabbath Day did not contradict God's laws, only the traditions of the rabbis. Jesus, therefore, dismissed the idea that his disciples were acting sinfully (Matt. 12:1-8).

God defines sin for us; man does not. We may not accuse of sin those whom God does not accuse. Our scruples may not bind the consciences of others, although they may choose to bind themselves for our sakes (1 John 3:4; Rom. 14).

4. We may not bind others with guidance which is not biblically substantiated

The lives of many people have been ruined by a new tyranny exercised by those who claim the authority of the Holy Spirit to guide others as to their marriages, jobs — almost everything. 'God has told me that you should...' has become the new authority, and is a road to spiritual bondage and a route of great danger.

What is needed is not the guidance of the self-proclaimed seer, but the direction of God to those who pray and study his Word. Few stories in the Bible are more tragic than that of the man of God from Judah who died because he followed *what someone else claimed* was God's word to him rather than *what he knew* was God's word to him (1 Kings 13:11-32). We ought to follow the certainties of Scripture, not the claimants of superior knowledge.

The Scriptures are sufficient, and this doctrine is important because it both safeguards God's truth, enabling us to know where to go for his Word, and secures our Christian liberty over against those who would take us captive to do their will, for only God is the Lord of conscience. Having God's recorded revelation in his Word, why should we turn to man-made chaff? Let us rather cling to the Bible, though all else be taken, for in the sure and certain Word of God we have all we need to please God. What more can we want?

Appendices

Two appendices have been added to this book to illustrate the practical outworking of Bob Sheehan's high view of Scripture. While in agreement with much of Dr Grudem's work, he felt it necessary to challenge the latter's view of continuing prophecy. He considered the Scriptures to be living and active, but also complete, and would not compromise this foundational biblical principle.

Bob Sheehan was above all a preacher and a pastor. His concern, throughout his ministry, was for the feeding and nurturing of the flock in his care, and for the preparation of young men for what he viewed as the highest calling of all — the ministry of the Word.

Because of this, we also felt it appropriate to include a second appendix: the text of one of his lectures to his students at the monthly seminary which he and others began at Welwyn Evangelical Church. This lecture shows how his high view of the triune God and of the Scriptures permeated his life and ministry. Throughout, Bob Sheehan's grasp of the original languages and his attention to every detail of the divine Word are seen. It is our hope that this lecture will inspire others to take the study of the Scriptures seriously and to dedicate all that they do and all that they are to the glory of God.

The publishers

Appendix I
Continuing prophecy

The first characteristic is that prophecy is God speaking. It is infallible... Secondly, we note the characteristic of supernaturalism in connection with true prophecy... The third note characteristic of all true God-given prophecy is the note of divine urgency... Fourthly, we must record that the prophets and prophecies always had to be tested in a stringent way.

Victor Budgen

No level of prophecy is introduced by 'I think the Lord is suggesting something like this'. To speak thus is not to speak prophecy at all.

Sinclair Ferguson

No further inspired, authoritative communications come to people other than those that are found in the Bible.

O. Palmer Robertson

Appendix I
Continuing prophecy:
A response to Wayne Grudem

The publication of Dr Grudem's *The Gift of Prophecy in 1 Corinthians*[1] in 1982 first suggested to the Christian public in general that there were two types of prophet and prophecy mentioned in the Bible. The first, best illustrated by the Old Testament prophets, involved authoritative speech with the introductory formula 'Thus says the Lord' and consisted of God's very words. The second, best illustrated by the New Testament prophets, did not use this formula and involved an initial revelation from the Spirit expressed in human words. The first type was infallible prophecy; the second was fallible prophecy.

The recent publication of Dr Grudem's *Systematic Theology*[2] has renewed the debate because he devotes twelve pages (pp. 1049-61) to a defence of continuing prophecy. What are his arguments and are they valid?

1. The use of the phrase 'Thus says the Lord...'

Dr Grudem argues that the standard Old Testament formula, 'Thus says the Lord', so distinctive of prophecies which were authoritative and infallible, is 'nowhere spoken in the New Testament by any prophets in the New Testament churches'

(p. 1055). Therefore the prophets had a different authority and level of accuracy.

Dr Grudem knows his Bible well enough to expect an immediate challenge. Did not the New Testament prophet Agabus introduce his New Testament prophecy with 'Thus says the Holy Spirit'? (Acts 21:11). Dr Grudem acknowledges that it 'is true that Agabus uses a similar phrase' (p. 1056).

In his two cited works, Dr Grudem gives five possible solutions to this problem. In 1982 he preferred the fourth solution; in 1994 he gives a new answer.

In 1982 the four solutions were, in summary:

1. Luke's reporting was confused.

2. Agabus was equivalent in authority to the Old Testament prophets (the historic position which Grudem opposes).

3. It is permissible to preface fallible prophecy with the formula 'Thus says the Lord' reserved in the Old Testament for infallible prophecy. Dr Grudem rejects this solution because, '"Thus says the Lord" is used too frequently in the Septuagint as a messenger formula for those who claimed a divine authority of actual words to make this solution likely.'[3] We need to take special note of this statement because it will become very important when we consider the fifth solution proposed by Dr Grudem.

4. 'Agabus, perhaps in trying to imitate the OT prophets or other NT prophets who claimed a divine authority of actual words, wrongly used an introductory formula which was inappropriate to his status as a prophet with lesser authority.'[4] This was Dr Grudem's preferred solution in 1982. Agabus had ideas above his station and used the formula incorrectly.

In his *Systematic Theology*, Dr Grudem has changed his ground entirely. Although he still accepts that 'Thus says the Lord' is the common Old Testament phrase preceding the very words of God (pp. 1050, 1055) and that 'Agabus uses a similar phrase' (p. 1056), he now argues that the words 'Thus says' are used by Christian writers just after the time of the New Testament 'to introduce very general paraphrases or greatly expanded interpretations of what is being reported... The phrase can mean, "This is generally what the Holy Spirit is saying to us" ' (p. 1056).

What an amazing transition! 'Thus says the Lord' once meant that the words which followed are the very words of God, but by the time the New Testament had just been completed it meant, 'This is the Holy Spirit's general idea'!

The fact is, however, that the allusions to early Christian literature cited by Dr Grudem to prove his case do nothing of the sort. His first reference is to Ignatius' *Epistle to the Philadelphians* 7:1-2 (p. 1056). In its context, Ignatius is referring to his visit to the Philadelphians and what he had taught them about church order. He recalls, 'I cried out when I was with you, I spoke with a great voice, with God's own voice... I had no knowledge of this from any human being, but the Spirit was preaching, and saying this.' Does Ignatius' claim to speak with God's own voice, that his teaching was the Spirit preaching and his use of the statement 'saying this' (equivalent to 'thus says') suggest he believed he was speaking authoritatively, or giving a general idea? Let the reader judge!

Dr Grudem's three citations from *the Epistle of Barnabas* 6:8; 9:2,5 (p.1056) are even less supportive of his claim. Barnabas 6:8 reads, 'What does the other prophet Moses say to them, "Behold thus says the Lord, enter into the good land which the Lord swore that he would give to Abraham, Isaac and Jacob and inherit it, a land flowing with milk and honey." '

This is a quotation of parts of Exodus 33:1-3. It is not a general idea in fallible words which could mislead!

In Barnabas 9:2 the formula 'Thus says the Lord' is used in the context of quotations from Psalms, Isaiah and Jeremiah. In Barnabas 9:5, 'Thus says the Lord' is used in a quotation from Jeremiah 4:3-4. Let the reader judge whether using 'Thus says the Lord' in contexts which gather quotations and allusions from Holy Scripture gives the phrase the loose meaning, 'This is generally what the Holy Spirit is saying to us,' as Dr Grudem claims, or whether it retains its usual authoritative meaning derived from its Old Testament use. Dr Grudem, I respectfully submit, has not proved his case, but rather undermined it by his suggestions.

Most significant of all, however, is the fact that our Lord introduces all his letters to the churches of Revelation by using the very same formula (Rev. 2:1,8,12,18; 3:1,7,14). Surely our Lord did not mean, 'This is the general idea of what I want to say to you, although it may not be entirely accurate,' did he? Yet that is what Dr Grudem would like the introductory phrase to mean!

The introductory formula used by Agabus and our Lord is the destruction of Dr Grudem's new idea of dual level prophets and prophecy, not its demonstration.

2. The relative roles of prophets and apostles

Secondly, Dr Grudem argues that the Old Testament prophets were replaced by the New Testament apostles and, therefore, the New Testament prophets must have had another role (p. 1050).

Of course, we have no desire to undermine the authority of the New Testament apostles, nor to deny their unique role in the Christian church. They did have an undoubted authority, even over the New Testament prophets (1 Cor. 14:37) because the apostles had all truth, whereas the prophets were only granted a partial understanding of the truth.

Nevertheless, the New Testament prophets are closely associated with the apostles in a manner that is not true of anyone else. Together they are the recipients of the mystery of Christ (Eph. 3:5) and are the foundation of the church (Eph. 2:20).

In both of his cited works, Dr Grudem seeks to undermine the significance of these verses. He asserts that it is grammatically possible (and it is) that in Ephesians 2:20 and 3:5 the Greek should be read not as 'apostles *and* prophets', but as 'apostles *who were* prophets' (p. 1052). In this way the apostle-prophets received revelation and are the foundation of the church, and these passages have nothing to do with the secondary, fallible type of prophet which Dr Grudem posits.

However, what is grammatically *possible* is not always contextually *probable*! In Ephesians 4:11 apostles and prophets are indisputably distinct groups. Why would Paul in one letter be so confusing as to write of apostle-prophets (a category of person nowhere else so defined in Scripture!) and then go on to write of apostles and prophets who were distinct? Indeed, Dr Grudem himself acknowledges that 'The words prophet and prophecy ...[were] not the ordinary terminology used for the apostles' (p.1051).

In a lengthy footnote (p.1051, note 4), Dr Grudem acknowledges that his suggested grammatical interpretation of these verses may not be correct but, amazingly, asserts that, in any case, 'I do not think that Eph. 2:20 has much relevance to the entire discussion of the nature of the gift of prophecy.' Yet he recognizes that, however we understand the prophets in Ephesians 2:20 and 3:5, 'These prophets are ones who provided the foundation of the church, and therefore these are prophets who spoke infallible words.' This concession is remarkable! He now acknowledges that there could be New Testament prophets who spoke infallible words and who are part of the foundation on which the church is built.

Grasp what is being said! The prophets of Ephesians 2:20 and 3:5 prophesied infallibly. Yet they do not have *much relevance to the entire discussion of the nature of the gift of prophecy*! It is an interesting procedure to seek to undermine or declare irrelevant those verses which contradict the theory being posited!

3. The meaning of the word 'prophet' in New Testament times

Thirdly, Dr Grudem argues that by New Testament times the meaning of the words 'prophet' and 'prophecy' had changed. Whereas in Old Testament days a prophet was 'one who speaks God's very words', by New Testament days it meant 'one who speaks on the basis of some external influence'.

To support his contention, Dr Grudem lists six examples from secular Greek usage, contemporary to the New Testament age, in which philosophers, teachers, botanists, medical 'quacks' and written history are all referred to as 'prophets'. But what does this prove? Only that in the secular Greek world the word 'prophet' had a very wide meaning, being used for almost anyone or anything that claimed to speak with authority. To claim to speak with authority is not the same as claiming to speak on the basis of some external influence, as Dr Grudem contends.

It is also difficult to see why, if the *secular* use of the word meant someone who spoke with authority, the *biblical* use must be identical. What was more influential on the New

Testament meaning of words — the Old Testament or secular Greek? Surely the Old Testament!

Dr Grudem presses his case by trying to demonstrate that this secular use is found in the New Testament. His trawl of New Testament evidence produces only two examples: the soldiers who hit our Lord called on him to prophesy (Luke 22:64) and Paul described the Cretan poet Epimenides as a prophet (Titus 1:12).

Let us weigh the evidence. Is the use of a word on the lips of sadistic, pagan soldiers to determine its normal biblical usage? When a young person today calls something 'wicked', meaning that it is really good, does that mean that modern Christian books mean by 'wicked' something to be commended?

Why did Paul refer to Epimenides as a Cretan prophet? Was it because Paul believed that Epimenides was a man divinely inspired with authoritative words? Not at all! Was it because his people considered him divinely inspired? Yes, it was! Not only did Plutarch consider him one of the seven wise men of the ancient world, but Plato described him as 'that divinely inspired Epimenides'.[5] Paul used the word 'prophet' to describe a man considered to be divinely inspired.

We have seen that in secular usage the Greeks did refer to someone who spoke authoritatively as a 'prophet'. They also referred to some as 'prophets' because they considered them to be divinely inspired. In the Old Testament, however, to be a prophet was more than to claim to speak with authority. By his examples, Dr Grudem has failed to prove his contention that in the New Testament, 'Commonly the words prophet and prophecy were used of ordinary Christians who spoke not with absolute divine authority but simply to report something that God had laid on their hearts or brought to their minds' (p.1051). The evidence he has produced proves no such thing!

4. The authority of New Testament prophets and prophecy

Dr Grudem's final argument is that there is evidence in the New Testament that the authority of New Testament prophets and prophecy was not particularly great at all. 'This ordinary gift of prophecy had authority less than that of the Bible, and even less than that of recognized Bible teaching in the church' (p.1051f.).

The statement that prophets had less authority in the church than Bible teachers is a strange conclusion when we consider that in the list of gifts prophets are always placed *after* apostles and *before* teachers (1 Cor. 12:28; Eph. 4:11). When the church had its true prophets, they had a proper position, under the apostles but before the teachers (Acts 13:1).

The reason for Dr Grudem's order is not biblical but pragmatic. Harsh experience of the realities concerning modern prophets has taught him that when the so-called prophets begin to run the church the Bible teachers are sidelined. Hence his need to devote a section of his *Systematic Theology* to advising church leaders on how to control the prophets they unleash! (pp. 1060-61).

Dr Grudem uses two texts to show that New Testament prophecies were of a mixed nature in their content, resembling the infamous curate's egg, which was good in parts and rotten in others! The proof texts are 1 Thessalonians 5:19-21, where the church is exhorted not to despise prophesying, to test everything and to hold on to what is good, and 1 Corinthians 14:29, where the prophets are allowed to speak and the others are exhorted to judge, or weigh.

Neither text, however, proves the point. The reason for testing all prophecies was not to distinguish in an individual prophecy between the good parts and the bad, but to distinguish between those that came from God and those that were spurious.

Lest it should be claimed that the origin of a prophecy would be obvious, let us note that 1 Corinthians 12:1-3 tells us that some people, claiming to be inspired of God, were actually declaring our Lord to be anathema! Paul had to tell the Corinthians that this could not be of God! Some people, when obsessed with the supernatural, leave all their powers of discernment at the church door!

In 2 Thessalonians 2:2, Paul had to issue a warning against prophecies which declared that the Day of the Lord had already arrived, and condemn them as false. It was the phenomenon of *false* prophecies, not of *mixed* prophecies, which required tests to be made. Even in Old Testament days there were tests to be applied to those who had prophesied (Deut. 13:1-5; 18:21-22).

What of 1 Corinthians 14:29? What are the others to 'judge' (AV) or 'weigh' (NIV)? It is reprehensible that the NIV supplies the words 'what is said' after the verb 'weigh', even though they do not appear in a single Greek manuscript. This translator's addition is supported by Dr Grudem but it is an imposition on the original.

The Greek verb is *diakrino*. It is found frequently in the New Testament to refer to distinctions made between *people*. God made no discrimination between the Jews and the Gentiles when he gave both the Spirit (Acts 15:9). James condemned those Christians who discriminated in their welcome and treatment in the church between the rich and the poor (James 2:3-4).

Paul's use of this verb in 1 Corinthians is, of course, particularly significant. God had discriminated between the Corinthians and others by his actions (4:7). In disputes among Christians other Christians should discriminate between the contending parties (6:5).

For this reason, when we consider 1 Corinthians 14:29, the discrimination to which we are called is not between *messages* (as Dr Grudem contends) but between *messengers*. False and true prophets had to be distinguished.

Agabus again!

In contending for a mixed prophecy, Dr Grudem uses as his main proof texts passages that concern Agabus (Acts 21:4,10-11). According to Dr Grudem, Agabus, who has already been subjected to five varying interpretations, is under scrutiny again, because his prophecy was inaccurate in its details and somewhat erroneous (p.1052).

According to Acts 21:11, Agabus prophesied (if we translate it rather literally): 'The man whose belt this is, in this way the Jews will bind in Jerusalem and will deliver him into the hands of the Gentiles.' When Paul arrived in Jerusalem he was attacked by a Jewish mob, rescued by the intervention of the Romans, and bound by order of the Roman soldiers (Acts 21:30-33; 22:29). If the Romans bound him, not the Jews, and the Romans rescued him, rather than his being delivered up to them, was not Agabus, strictly speaking, inaccurate? Indeed, is 'strictly speaking' strong enough?

Great care has to be taken with prophetic language. As a premillennialist, Dr Grudem would, of course, want to emphasize literalism in detail, but prophetic literalism has led to all sorts of problems in interpreting Scriptures.

The comments of R. C. H. Lenski, written before anyone had ever heard of mixed prophecies and, therefore, made with no relationship to the debate in view, are interesting: 'The girdle was used to bind up the long, loose outer robe when one walked rapidly or worked; the binding of both feet and hands, then, meant that for a time Paul would not be able to travel or to work at will as he had done heretofore. Any work that he now did would be done as a prisoner.'[6]

For Dr Lenski, the prophecy was a symbolic statement of restriction, not a foretelling of literal events. Paul's work would be hindered, firstly, by the Jews, then by the Gentiles, as together they imprisoned him. Hence there are no inaccuracies!

Those who would be quick to demand that the prophecy must be fulfilled literally have their own problems. Agabus took Paul's belt and bound him with it and prophesied that the would be bound 'in this way'. In fact, he was bound by the Romans with two chains, not a belt (Acts 21:33).

On what sure basis can it be stated that the Jews did not tie up Paul with his belt as they attacked him and dragged him out of the city? (Acts 21:30-31). A restrained victim would be much more vulnerable than one who had free hands and legs to resist! Did not the Jews deliver up Paul to the Romans? When they saw the soldiers arrive they stopped beating him and he was arrested. Their victim became the responsibility of the Romans (Acts 21:32-36).

My own preference is to follow the lead given by Dr Lenski. There is no biblical requirement to impose literalism on the fulfilment of prophecies. Dr Grudem has not, therefore, demonstrated that Agabus is an example of a prophet of the mixed variety.

Disobeying the Spirit?

The last string to Dr Grudem's bow is Acts 21:4, where Paul was told through the Spirit not to go to Jerusalem, but went. Candidly, this passage poses a difficulty of interpretation for everyone.

Dr Grudem's simple comment is that 'This seems to be a reference to prophecy directed towards Paul, but Paul disobeyed it.' Notice the hesitancy of 'seems'. He continues, 'He would never have done this if this prophecy contained God's very words and had authority equal to Scripture' (p. 1052).

In his earliest cited work, Dr Grudem explained that he believed that the Holy Spirit had given a warning of the sufferings which Paul would face (cf. Acts 20:23), but these prophets had added their own interpretation to it, which was a false command not to go to Jerusalem. Paul detected this and so ignored it (pp. 78,149).

Therefore, to Dr Grudem 'through the Spirit' meant as a result of a message received from the Spirit. 'Through the Spirit' referred only to the source of the message, and not to the message as it was finally given. This was, therefore, not a prophecy with good and bad mixed in it, but a totally misleading prophecy, a false prophecy. The humans who delivered the message distorted the Spirit's meaning. Again, therefore, Dr Grudem has changed his ground in his two books and has adopted a more extreme position in his later work.

Many commentators who would not accept Dr Grudem's idea of mixed prophecy accept that in this passage 'through the Spirit' means 'speaking by the spirit of prophecy', which they identify with the Holy Spirit.[7]

Also, many accept that the disciples received a message of troubles for Paul at Jerusalem and drew a false inference from it. John Calvin comments, 'It is no wonder that those who are strong in the gift of prophecy are sometimes lacking in judgement and courage.'[8]

Dr Alexander comments that 'This was not a divine command to Paul, but an inference of the disciples from the fact, which was revealed to them, that Paul would be in great danger.'[9]

Dr Lenski agrees: 'The disciples understood the Spirit's word as a warning which they should transmit to Paul.'[10]

Similarly, Dr Robertson comments, 'The Spirit reveals the trials Paul would undergo, and the brothers took it on themselves to attempt to persuade him not to proceed.'[11]

What, then, is the difference between Dr Grudem's latest interpretation of this passage and the other interpreters quoted? All are agreed that the Spirit had revealed the dangers awaiting Paul and that the disciples, with no ill intent, but perhaps out of a misguided love for Paul (cf. Matt. 16:22), had drawn a false inference. All are agreed that Paul felt entirely free to reject this inference.

The difference is that Dr Grudem would call this false inference 'prophecy' and see it as part and parcel of normal prophetic life to have these mistakes. The rest would see it as an inference from prophecies, but not view the inference itself as prophecy. The difference is the chasm between the hit-and-miss philosophy of prophets and prophecy espoused by Dr Grudem and the certainties of prophets and prophecy declared by historic Christianity.

Conclusion

It is my contention that Dr Grudem has failed to prove his case for a continuing type of secondary, mixed prophecy. His arguments do not corroborate his thesis. Until better evidence is produced the curate's egg of pseudo-prophecy must be ignored for the wholesome food of God's infallible Word.

Appendix II
Sermon preparation

Teachers have a separate responsibility of their own, which is to expound the Scripture that there may always be a good and sound understanding of it, and that the same may have its force and continue in the church, so that heresies and false opinions may not spread, but that the faith may abide firm and sure above all things.

John Calvin

The man who handles the word of the truth properly does not change, pervert, mutilate or distort it, neither does he use it with a wrong purpose in mind. On the contrary, he prayerfully interprets Scripture in the light of Scripture. He courageously, yet lovingly, applies its glorious meaning to concrete conditions and circumstances, doing this for the glory of God, the conversion of sinners, and the edification of believers.

William Hendriksen

One of the first and most important duties of a gospel minister is the investigation of truth. If he fails here he fails everywhere. And truth, gospel truth, is of a very peculiar character. It is not the result of cold and heartless speculation. It is not discovered by the mere power of intellect. It mocks the pride of the philosopher. But to the meek, humble, subdued mind of the sincere Christian, it spontaneously unveils its charms, and imparts its treasure. In a word, to the discovery of gospel truth, the chief requisite, the grand desideratum, is seriousness.

Daniel Dana

Appendix II
Sermon preparation

The man who is called of God to preach has to put his call into practice. In order to do this he has need of both general and specific preparation for preaching. General preparation refers to those things which put him in the correct spiritual and intellectual frame for preaching. Specific preparation means those things which pertain to a particular sermon, or series of sermons.

General preparation

The preacher's general preparation involves his spirit and his mind, in that order. Being intellectually equipped to preach is of no value if we are not spiritually ready. In the same way, although not to the same degree, to be spiritually healthy, yet intellectually barren, is highly undesirable.

1. Spiritual preparation

In his address to the Ephesian elders, Paul commanded them, 'Take heed to *yourselves* and ... the flock' (Acts 20:28). The order is not unimportant. The care for other souls depends on the care the preacher gives to his own soul. He who would teach others must first teach himself. He who sheds light must first have light. Whoever would draw others near to God should himself be near to God.

In the same vein, writing to Timothy, Paul wrote, 'Look to yourself and your teaching' (1 Tim. 4:16). What I am is even more important than what I teach. The teaching must be sound, but so must the preacher. What a terrible indictment it is when others must be warned only to listen to what a person says, but not to follow his practice! (Matt. 23:3).

A man's preparation for the pulpit begins with his own spiritual life. There is no special method of maintaining spirituality for the preacher. He is fundamentally no different from other men and women. His spiritual life will be sustained by Bible reading and prayer. It is pitiful to hear some men claim that they can safely neglect such things because, as ministers, they spend their time formally in such activities. Ministerial prayers and study will not make up for a lack of private prayer and study.

Great men of God, giants in the pulpit, confirm this. C. H. Spurgeon devoted a chapter of the volume containing his lectures to his ministerial students to 'The preacher's private prayer'. He began this chapter with what he considered to be a self-evident truth: 'Of course the preacher is above all others distinguished as a man of prayer. He prays as an ordinary Christian, else he were a hypocrite. He prays more than ordinary Christians, else he were disqualified for the office he has undertaken.'[1]

The preacher's prayer life cannot just be a little here and a little there, no more than paying our respects to the idea of prayer. Rather, as Dr Lloyd-Jones observes, 'Prayer is vital to the life of the preacher... Prayer should be going on throughout the day... Be always in a prayerful condition. As you are walking along a road, or while you are in your study, you turn frequently to God in prayer... Always respond to every impulse to pray... From every standpoint the minister, the preacher, must be a man of prayer.'[2]

Alongside prayer, the reading of the Bible is the next essential in the preacher's life. Such reading should be systematic, and for the good of the preacher's own soul. Merely to read Scripture as a means to preparing sermons is a major mistake. The preacher needs his Bible as a Christian before he needs it as a preacher.

Reading and praying for my own spiritual benefit, listening to God in his Word and speaking to God in prayer are vital elements of true pulpit preparation. They give the spirit its tone, so that the preacher not only receives benefit for himself, but goes on to be a benefit to others.

Failure to maintain his 'Quiet Time' is a major tragedy, not only for the preacher himself, but also for his hearers. His spiritual decline will be the harbinger of their spiritual starvation.

2. Intellectual preparation

Over and above any reading that needs to be done for the preparation of a specific sermon, the preacher needs to be a reader. Such reading will impart information, generate thought, provide illustrations and generally equip the preacher's mind to be full of fresh and fertile ideas. Those who do not constantly read new material soon become like a record stuck in a groove — merely repetitious and predictable. Of them it is soon said, 'Ten thousand thousand are their texts, but all their sermons one!'

Areas of reading

Three areas of reading are particularly important to the preacher in his general reading.

Theology

Preachers can never outgrow the need to read theology. The preacher's mind continually needs to be stimulated with a deeper understanding of the great truths of Scripture. At best, seminary courses can lay a modest foundation for understanding these truths, but there is a lifelong development of that foundational bedrock that is essential if the preacher is to be equipped to explain and apply the truth in an ever-changing situation.

Church history

Undoubtedly, we will fail to properly understand the present unless we understand the past. There are virtually no new heresies; they are just the old ones dressed up in a new way. Church history guards us from many errors and enthusiasms to which we could so easily succumb if we are ignorant about the past.

Applied theology

By 'applied theology' I mean reading the works of those men who were masters in the care of the soul and in the solution of spiritual problems. I do not mean by this the plethora of modern counselling books, with their simplistic solutions and case histories. I mean the real pastoral masters, the Puritans.

Other areas of reading have their place, but these three areas are more important than any others. There are thousands of second-rate books, but we only have enough time to read the best. It is better to read one good book thoroughly than many smaller books scantily.

The effects produced by his reading

The preacher's reading may be defined not in mere categories — theology, church history, applied theology — but also in terms of the effects produced.

Books which expand the mind

The tendency of the day is to read little, simple paperbacks which aim to make easy everything, however profound. 'Easy-to-read' books do have a place, but not as the staple diet of the preacher. He must preach simply but study deeply, so that he has the answers to those problems which perplex his congregation and does not prove just as ignorant as they are on the matters which disturb them!

Among the mind-expanding books that ought to be read during a lifetime's ministry are the works of John Calvin, John Owen, Jonathan Edwards, James Henley Thornwell, Robert Louis Dabney, Charles Hodge, B. B. Warfield and John Murray.

Books which inspire and inform

Regardless of whether a preacher liked history at school or not, he ought to like church history. It is the story of God's dealings with the church and is both informative and inspiring. God's use of men and movements in the past is invaluable for the present. Good biographies and the autobiographies of men who have been greatly used as preachers are particularly useful.

Among those books which inspire and inform are the major biographies on Luther, Calvin, Whitefield, Edwards, Dabney, Thornwell, Palmer, Spurgeon and Lloyd-Jones.

Books which expand the soul

The writers who expand the mind do not always warm the
heart, although many do. Informational books often inspire
but do not search us, although some can. We need, therefore,
more searching books which will rebuke, correct and instruct
us in our spiritual pilgrimage. The Puritans and their heirs are
masters in this matter.

Not all the Puritans are easy to read, but preachers should
at least try some of the easier writers, e.g. William Bridge,
Jeremiah Burroughs, Thomas Watson, John Bunyan, Robert
Traill and Richard Sibbes. The more adventurous might go on
to Thomas Goodwin, Stephen Charnock and John Owen.

Among the 'heirs of the Puritans', great benefit can be derived by reading anything written by C. H. Spurgeon and especially three of Dr Lloyd-Jones' expositions: the Sermon on
the Mount, Romans and Ephesians.

The need for self-discipline

To find time for this general reading is going to be one of the
most difficult things in the preacher's life. After many years in
the ministry one of the greatest regrets of many preachers is
that they have read so much that was not worth reading, and
that so much has been read scantily without proper absorption
and thought. Merely to read and not to assimilate is of little
use. Quantity can never replace quality.

The preacher has responsibilities to his family, to the state
of which he is a citizen and as a church member in general. He
must, however, decide what he needs to do to fulfil his pri-
mary calling, that of preacher of the Word, and must not let
other things fill the time which he ought to give to that work,
including his general preparation.

If this reading is to be accomplished, then there needs to be a large amount of self-discipline. In an earthly sense the preacher is his own 'boss'. Without someone over him to order his life, he can easily fritter away time.

Our temptation to fritter away the time perhaps needs to be compared with the ideal that the Puritans set themselves. Richard Baxter wrote:

> 1. To redeem time is to see that we cast none of it away in vain; but use every minute of it as a most precious thing, and spend it wholly in the way of duty.
>
> 2. That we be not only doing good, but doing the best and greatest good which we are able and have a call to do.
>
> 3. That we do not only the best things, but do them in the best manner and in the greatest measure, and do as much good as we possibly can.'[3]

Those who are going to enter the ministry of preaching need the highest ideals and the strictest of self-discipline. Those of us who are in it need to repent of what we have done that is wrong and set about doing what needs to be done with renewed vigour.

Specific preparation

The preacher has to have a definite aim in view in his preaching. His intention may be summarized as a desire to present an appropriate part of God's truth to his hearers, in dependence on the Holy Spirit, in order to effect a spiritual change in them. The preacher is not merely a lecturer imparting knowledge. He has the salvation and sanctification of his hearers in view.

He wants them to be different people after they have heard him from what they were before he began to preach.

Of course, the preacher by himself has no way of bringing about change in his hearers. That is the work of the Holy Spirit. The preacher may preach in 'word only'. He needs to preach with power, conviction and presence of the Holy Spirit (1 Thess. 1:5). As God's Spirit is as free as the wind, the preacher must learn to rely on him to bless the Word in its delivery and its effect (John 3:8).

Finding the appropriate text

It is sometimes assumed that as 'All Scripture is God-breathed and ... profitable', the preacher may preach at any time from any portion of God's Word. This is a misunderstanding. The fact that all Scripture is profitable does not mean that every, or any, scripture is profitable on every, or any, occasion. Rather, it should be the preacher's concern to preach what God wants him to preach for the good of his hearers on each occasion that he preaches. He should have a sense that he is preaching the correct truth for that occasion, the very truth that God has guided him to preach.

Of course, it is true that God can just as much guide a preacher to preach a series, or through a biblical book, as he can to preach a particular text. God is not limited in the direction he may give merely to guidance for a single sermon!

The key point is that the Spirit of God must guide the preacher to the text, or texts, or book, that he should preach. If the preacher takes this seriously he will never become a mere manufacturer of sermons, producing the weekly sermons with the regularity and tedium of a sausage machine!

The preacher must seek God for what he ought to preach. He will not ignore the situation that his congregation faces, or particular doctrines, or practices, which need to be emphasized in his opinion, but his sermons will be determined by a sense of divine guidance, rather than topicality or personal prejudice.

The determination of what ought to be preached is inevitably and vitally linked to the ministry of prayer. By prayer he determines God's will. He takes the biblical injunction seriously that the man who lacks wisdom asks God and that God gives wisdom ungrudgingly (James 1:5).

Sometimes God makes clear what ought to be preached on a certain occasion very quickly and clearly. On other occasions, especially before beginning a new series, numerous options will be prayerfully considered and reconsidered, until ultimately peace is granted that a particular series is correct, or that a particular text ought to be expounded.

The key to text choice is prayer — persistent and regular prayer, so that the preacher knows that he is preaching the correct sermon every time he preaches. The attitude that says that 'Any old sermon will do,' produces preaching of a similar quality!

Understanding the text

If we are to see the wonderful things which are in God's Word, then we need to have our eyes opened by the Spirit of God. He is the Spirit of wisdom and revelation, by whom we receive spiritual discernment. If the key to text choice is prayer, it is also the key to spiritual understanding (Ps. 119:18; Eph. 1:17-18).

Traditionally it is said of the apostle John that when he was very old he used to be carried into church. Each Lord's Day he would be asked whether he had anything to say to the congregation. Every time he simply said, 'Love one another.'

Somewhat exasperated, the people asked why he always repeated the same command. His reply was that they needed to
love one another! For the preacher the story could be adapted
and the often-repeated command would become, 'Pray.'

There are at least four stages in the understanding of a particular text.

1. Understanding the text itself

Each text of Scripture is composed of individual words,
phrases, clauses and sentences. We need to try to understand
the English text before us in the light of the original text behind it.

There are various aids, even for those who do not have
proficiency in the original languages, which enable the preacher
to gain a clearer understanding of his text. He must not misuse
them, quoting them in a way which gives the impression that
he knows languages that he does not! But he should use all
aids which are available. The meaning of the words in our text
can be discovered more accurately by the use of word
dictionaries.

2. Understanding the context

Each verse is set in its own context. It is a dangerous thing to
preach a text out of context. Almost anything can be made of
a text such as 'Everyone who loves has been born of God and
knows God,' if it is preached out of its context!

It is in the understanding of the context of a verse that the
use of commentaries becomes especially important. There are
two dangers with commentaries. On the one hand, they can
do all our thinking for us and we can accept their teaching
blindly. In the wrong hands they are an aid to laziness. On the
other hand, we can despise them and adopt the conceit that,
although we expect the Holy Spirit to guide us as we study the

text, we do not accept that he could ever have guided anyone else! What God has helped others to see is seen for our benefit as well as theirs! In addition to commentaries many issues can be clarified by reference to a good Bible Dictionary.

3. Understanding the wider context

One of the main concerns of liberal thinking is to find as many as possible conflicting lines of thought, or theologies, in the Bible. The Law is set over against the Prophets, Paul over against the Jerusalem church and the apostles against the Jews, etc. The fundamental principle of evangelical theology is the internal consistency of Scripture. The main parts form one consistent testimony to truth.

The implication of internal consistency in the exposition of Scripture is that no part of Scripture can be correctly interpreted if it is interpreted as contradicting another. Contradictory interpretations must be wrong. This does not require the abolition of antinomy or paradox. Two truths may be held in tension with each other, but not in contradiction of each other. Jesus may be revealed in one text as human and in another as divine, but he may not be revealed in one text as human and in another as not human! The treatment of justification by Paul and James must therefore be interpreted in a complementary, and not a contradictory, way.

To gain an understanding of how a particular verse and its context fit into the whole biblical picture and are consistent with it is a role that commentaries and good works of theology supply.

4. Understanding the relevance

Once we have understood what the text means, we must understand its importance, relevance and application to the congregation. This is one of the most important, yet most neglected, parts of sermon preparation. The main components of this part of sermon preparation are neither reading nor writing, but thinking and meditating.

Having understood the truth of the text, we have to ask, 'Why does this text matter?' The earlier we have done our basic study into the context and meaning of the text, the better. We now have time to think, pray and 'chew over' in our minds the text we want to expound. We can do that in our studies, as we are walking, shaving, taking a bath — anywhere! If we have memorized the text, then all the better!

The more we can know our text thoroughly and feel it to be our 'burden', which we carry with us everywhere and meditate upon regularly, the easier will be our preparation and presentation of the sermon we intend to preach.

The exhortation to meditation which is found in the First Psalm is the key to understanding the text. As we understand why a text is important for us and does us good, we will understand why it is important for others and will do them good.

Orderly presentation

Preaching should not be a ramble but should have an orderly presentation. To attain this the preacher must understand his text and his aim. Inability to express an idea clearly usually signifies a failure to understand. At the outset it again needs to be emphasized that prayerfulness over presentation is essential. Even Paul asked the Ephesians to pray that words might be given him (Eph. 6:19).

Every sermon needs a basic structure: an introduction, a series of propositions which are related to each other in the logical order, followed by a climactic conclusion. An unstructured sermon is as unpalatable as a three-course meal, all of which has been thrown onto a single plate for consumption! Many a sermon is ineffective because it has no skeleton to aid the memory of the hearer and appears as a pile of unshaped flesh!

The introduction

The introduction to a sermon is important because it is the means by which the preacher attracts the attention of his hearers and encourages them to pay attention to what he is saying. The more sleepy, or indifferent, or hostile the audience, the more important a good beginning becomes. The preacher wants the members of the congregation to say to themselves, 'This is going to be worth my time hearing.'

Of course the introduction has to be a true introduction to the subject in hand, and not merely an unrelated joke or story to 'soften up the audience'. Such tendencies towards acting and audience manipulation should be avoided. The preacher is not an entertainer, or a storyteller, but an ambassador of Christ.

The way a man introduces his sermon will reflect his own character and, therefore, there is not one correct way of introducing it, but an introduction is necessary. The variety of forms the introduction may take can be seen by a comparison of different preachers from various ages, and by the recognition that different congregations require different introductions. A man preaching to a regularly gathered congregation will introduce his material, especially if he is going through a series, in a different way from a man preaching a one-off sermon, or to an especially gathered congregation. Preaching for teaching will often be introduced in a different way from preaching for evangelistic purposes. To teach a regular congregation is not the same as to evangelize the unconverted.

However short or long the introduction is, it remains only the introduction. It must not be better than the main body of the sermon. No one would be particularly pleased with a meal with a superb first course and a miserable main dish! So with the sermon. The main body of teaching must be even better than the introduction.

The heart of the sermon

Having previously gained an understanding of the meaning and significance of the text, the truth of the text needs to be presented in a structured and logical form.

Some seek to impose a universal structure on the sermon: it must have three points. My sentiment is, 'A plague on their uniformity!' As a general guide, but no more, each sermon should have as many points as the preacher and the congregation could reasonably be expected to remember.

Simplicity

The fact that we want the congregation to be able both to remember and to understand the main teaching we are giving them means that we must strive for the simplest structure explained in the simplest language. Why should we admire preachers who have headings to their sermon points that are a paragraph long, impossible to remember and incomprehensible to the children? Expressing ourselves clearly enough and simply enough for a child to understand our main points is important. We do not preach to display our great learning or familiarity with unusual vocabulary. We mortify our cleverness for the sake of clarity.

Logical order

This reasonable number of clearly stated points must be presented in a logical order. For example, if we are preaching on the love of God from eternity to eternity, then we need to begin with the evidence of that love in eternity past, then in present earthly history and finally in eternity to come. Any other order would be ludicrous!

If we are dealing with a passage containing things of varying importance, then we must work from the least important to the most significant. The creation of a climax is important. A sermon that climaxes in the middle and subsequently proceeds to an anticlimax is going to frustrate and bore a congregation.

Illustration

As the sermon proceeds through each point, appropriate illustrations should be used. Appropriate illustration is *fitting to the people addressed*. Adult congregations do not want perpetually to hear illustrations taken from the playground. Appropriate use of illustration is *suited to the subject matter*. The danger of inappropriate use of illustrations is to trivialize the profound.

The appropriate use of illustrations is simple and leaves the hearer with a clear understanding of the point behind the illustration. No preacher really wants to be remembered for his illustrations and for his message to be forgotten!

A great fund of illustrations will be built up by regular Bible reading. Further illustrations will be discovered by the reading of history and biography, and by being observant of everyday life. There is such a thing as living in the light of preaching — looking at everything from its opportunity to be used for illustration.

However, certain dangers also have to be avoided. Some preachers use far too many illustrations. They join scriptural texts together with stories, and little more. Other preachers use so many illustrations from their own experience that their sermons are one continual testimony rather than preaching of the Word! There are also preachers who feel that to be relevant they have to use illustrations from their own congregation, from the confidences that have been given to them and from sources that were not made known to be made public. This is not preaching; it is gossip!

Application

It is essential that every sermon should contain application. There are two main patterns in the New Testament, both of which the preacher will need to follow, depending on the type of text, or passage, which he is expounding.

The first pattern is that of Paul. The general structure of his epistles is a declaration of doctrine followed by an application of the doctrine taught. Sometimes this is the best method for preaching — explanation and application.

The second pattern is that of the general epistles. There explanation and application are consistently interwoven. As each point is explained, it is applied. This method is certainly helpful in retaining the attention of the hearers. If they feel constantly the relevance of what is being said, they are more likely to pay attention to it.

Again, the application has to be appropriate. Some applications have a suitability to all; others to specific groups. Both types of application have to be made.

Application has to be applied! Preachers sometimes expect the application to be obvious to the hearer, but generally, as the hearer has not done the same amount of study as the preacher on the text, the application has to be spelt out. The danger for the hearer is to assume that the preaching does not apply to himself but to someone else! He needs to be shown that it is relevant to him.

The conclusion

Preachers often have more difficulty with the conclusion to their sermons than anything else. Luther's maxim to young preachers, 'Stand up cheerily; speak up manfully; leave off speedily,' is easier said than done!

If the sermon has been constructed logically, and it has reached its climax in its final application, then not a word should be added to that climactic exhortation. It is good that we should leave our hearers with a pointed question, or a sincere exhortation, or a heartfelt plea, and do not let our sermon fade into silence. Let it blaze into a climax

The key elements in all sermon preparation are prayer, study, meditation and ordered structure. From this preparation in the study and in the mind, the preacher must then turn to preaching itself.

Notes

Chapter 3 — Special revelation
1. The Prayer of Azariah 15; 2 Baruch 85:3.
2. 1 Maccabees 9:27; 4:45-46; 14:41; Qumran Manual of Discipline I 9:11

Chapter 4 — Canonical Scripture and its authority
1. See chapter 2.
2. See chapter 3.
3. See R. L. Harris, *Inspiration and Canonicity of the Bible*, Zondervan, 1957, pp.168-9.
4. Quoted by R. Pache, *The Inspiration and Authority of Scripture*, Moody Press, 1974, p.163.
5. Quoted by F. F. Bruce, *The Canon of Scripture*, Chapter House, 1988, p.33.
6. R. K. Harrison, *Introduction to the Old Testament*, Tyndale Press, 1971, p.270.
7. Prologue to Ecclesiasticus in the Old Testament Apocrypha.
8. Quoted by Bruce, *The Canon of Scripture*, p.46.
9. 2 Maccabees 15:9; Harrison, *Introduction to the Old Testament*, p.276.
10. Bruce, *The Canon of Scripture*, pp.28,41.
11. R. T. France, *Jesus and the Old Testament*, Baker, 1982, pp.259-63.
12. Rimmer, quoted by R. P. Lightner, *The Saviour and the Scriptures*, Baker, 1978, p.28.
13. *Greek New Testament*, United Bible Societies, 1975, pp.900-903.
14. Referred to in J. Wenham, *Christ and the Bible*, IVP, 1979, p.145, note 2.
15. Quoted by Pache, *The Inspiration and Authority of Scripture*, p.164.
16. *Ibid.*, p.163.
17. G. F. Moore, *Judaism*, vol. I, p.239.
18. C. K. Barrett, *The Gospel According to Saint John*, SPCK, 1970, p.320.
19. B. B. Warfield, *Works*, Baker, 1981, vol. I, p.265.
20. Quoted by Pache, *The Inspiration and Authority of Scripture*, p.46.
21. J. N. D. Kelly, *Early Christian Doctrines*, A. & C. Black, 1968, p.31.
22. *Ibid.*, p.32.
23. *Ibid.*, p.33.
24. Bruce, *The Canon of Scripture*, p.258.

Chapter 5 — Attitudes to Scripture
1. *The New Columbian Encyclopaedia*, quoted by J. M. Boice, *The Foundations of Biblical Authority*, Zondervan, 1978, p.24.
2. Quoted by E. J. Young, *Thy Word is Truth*, Banner of Truth, 1968, p.227.
   The official English translation of Barth's works renders this passage as follows: 'If God was not ashamed of the fallibility of all the human words of the Bible, of their historical and scientific inaccuracies, their theological contradictions, the uncertainty of their tradition and, above all, their Judaism, but adopted and made use of these expressions in all their fallibility, we do not need to be ashamed when He wills to renew it to us in all its fallibility as witness...' (Karl Barth, *Church Dogmatics*, T. & T. Clark, 1956, vol. 1.2, p.531).
3. B. M. Palmer, *Theology of Prayer*, Sprinkle, 1980, pp.71-2.
4. See, e.g. G. L. Archer, *Encyclopaedia of Bible Difficulties*, Zondervan, 1982.

Chapter 6 — The original text of Scripture
1. For a further discussion of New Testament criticism see Bob Sheehan, *Which Version Now?*, Carey Publications.

Chapter 7 — The translation of Scripture
1. For a further discussion of the issue in this chapter see Bob Sheehan, *Which Version Now?*

Chapter 8 — The sufficiency of Scripture
1. J. I. Packer in J. W. Montgomery, *God's Inerrant Word*, Bethany Fellowhship, 1974, pp.48-9.
2. A. Dallimore, *George Whitefield*, Banner of Truth, 1980, vol. II, pp.167-9.
3. D. Dickson, *A Commentary on Psalms*, Banner of Truth, 1965, p.133.
4. M. Henry, *An Exposition of the Old and New Testaments*, Partridge & Oakey, 1848, p.140.
5. T. M'Crie, *The Life of John Knox*, Free Presbyterian Publications, 1978, p.284.
6. *Ibid.*, p.285.
7. C. H. Spurgeon, *Twelve Sermons on Holiness*, Reiner Publications, 1965, p.7.
8. Quoted by M. M. Knappen, *Tudor Puritanism*, University of Chicago Press, 1970, p.69.

Appendix I — Continuing prophecy
1. W. Grudem, *The Gift of Prophecy in 1 Corinthians*, University Press of America, 1982.
2. W. Grudem, *Systematic Theology*, IVP, 1994.
3. Grudem, *Gift of Prophecy*, p.82.
4. *Ibid.*
5. Information from W. Hendriksen, *1 & 2 Timothy and Titus*, Banner of Truth, 1972, pp.352-3.
6. R. C. H. Lenski, *The Interpretation of the Acts of the Apostles*, Augsburg, 1961, p.869.
7. J. Calvin, *Acts of the Apostles, 14-28*, Saint Andrew Press, 1966, p.193 and Lenski, *Interpretation of Acts*, p.862.
8. Calvin, *Acts of the Apostles, 14-28*, p.193.

9. J. A. Alexander, *A Commentary on the Acts of the Apostles,* Banner of Truth, 1984, vol. 12, p.260.
10. Lenski, *Interpretation of Acts,* p.10.
11. O. Palmer Robertson, *The Final Word,* Banner of Truth, 1993, p.112.

Appendix II — Sermon preparation
1. C. H. Spurgeon, *Lectures to my Students,* Marshall, Morgan and Scott, 1970, p.42.
2. D. M. Lloyd-Jones, *Preachers and Preaching,* Hodder and Stoughton, 1971, pp.169-71.
3. R. Baxter, *The Christian Directory,* Soli Deo Gloria, 1990, p.1231.

Index

Scripture index